Metro Revealed

Building Windows 8 Apps with HTML5 and JavaScript

Adam Freeman

Apress®

Metro Revealed: Building Windows 8 Apps with HTML5 and JavaScript

Copyright © 2012 by Adam Freeman

ISBN-13 (pbk): 978-1-4302-4488-2

ISBN-13 (electronic): 978-1-4302-4489-9

President and Publisher: Paul Manning
Lead Editor: Ewan Buckingham
Technical Reviewer: Fabio Claudio Ferracchiati
Editorial Board: Steve Anglin, Ewan Buckingham, Gary Cornell, Louise Corrigan, Morgan Ertel,
    Jonathan Gennick, Jonathan Hassell, Robert Hutchinson, Michelle Lowman, James Markham,
    Matthew Moodie, Jeff Olson, Jeffrey Pepper, Douglas Pundick, Ben Renow-Clarke, Dominic
    Shakeshaft, Gwenan Spearing, Matt Wade, Tom Welsh
Coordinating Editor: Jennifer L. Blackwell
Copy Editor: Kim Wimpsett
Compositor: SPi Global
Indexer: SPi Global
Artist: SPi Global
Cover Designer: Anna Ishchenko

Distributed to the book trade worldwide by Springer Science+Business Media New York, 233 Spring Street, 6th Floor, New York, NY 10013. Phone 1-800-SPRINGER, fax (201) 348-4505, e-mail orders-ny@springer-sbm.com, or visit www.springeronline.com.

For information on translations, please e-mail rights@apress.com, or visit www.apress.com.

Apress and friends of ED books may be purchased in bulk for academic, corporate, or promotional use. eBook versions and licenses are also available for most titles. For more information, reference our Special Bulk Sales–eBook Licensing web page at www.apress.com/bulk-sales.

Any source code or other supplementary materials referenced by the author in this text is available to readers at www.apress.com. For detailed information about how to locate your book's source code, go to www.apress.com/source-code.

Dedicated to my lovely wife, Jacqui Griffyth

– Adam Freeman

Contents at a Glance

Contents

Related Titles from Apress

Apress titles are available in print and electronic form at computer booksellers and electronic bookstores around the world. Many of the titles listed here are available or will be available soon on Apress.com on the Apress Alpha book program. Therein you can purchase a book, get chapters as they are developed and in the end you will get the final ebook – all for the price of a normal Apress ebook. It's a great way to get started as our authors create the books. Simply go to the book's page and click the yellow *Buy Alpha Book* button. Thereafter, you can go in at any time and download the latest additions to your ebook. Apress will notify you upon publication when the final ebook is available.

Upcoming publications include:

Available in May.
Metro Revealed: Building Windows 8 apps with XAML and C#

Available in June.
Pro C# and the .NET 4.5 Framework *6th Edition*

Available this spring.
WinRT Revealed
Pro WinRT using C# and XAML
978-1-4302-4515-5
Beginning Silverlight 5 in C# *4 Edition*

Available this summer.
Metro Style Application Recipes for Windows 8 in C#

Pro Windows 8 Development with XAML and C#
978-1-4302-4047-1

Pro Application Lifecycle Management with Visual Studio *2nd Edition*

Pro HTML5 Performance
978-1-4302-4524-7

Beginning HTML5 and CSS3

Foundation HTML5 with CSS3

Pro JavaScript for Web Apps

Beginning ASP.NET 4.5 in C#

Beginning ASP.NET 4.5 in VB

Ultra-Fast ASP.NET 4.5 *2nd Edition*

Beginning ASP.NET 4.5 Databases *3rd*

Beginning C# 2012 Databases *2nd Edition*

Illustrated C# 2012 *4 Edition*

Introducing .NET 4.5 *2nd Edition*

Pro WF 4.5

The Windows 8 Power Users Guide

Pro SQL Azure *2nd Edition*

Available this fall.
Beginning Metro Application Development in Windows 8 –XAML Edition
978-1-4302-4566-7

Pro Visual Studio 11

Beginning Windows 8 App Development
978-1-4302-4563-6

Pro HTML5 with Visual Studio 2012
978-1-4302-4638-1

Pro Business Metro Style Apps in XAML

Pro HTML5 Application Development

Pro ASP.NET MVC 4 *4 Edition.*

Pro ASP.NET 4.5 in C# *5th Edition*

Pro ASP.NET 4.5 in VB *5th Edition*

JavaScript Programmer's Reference
978-1-4302-4629-9

Pro WPF in C# 2012 *4 Edition*

Pro Windows 8 Development with HTML5 and JavaScript

Pro .Net Performance
978-1-4302-4458-5

Related published publications include:

Windows Azure Platform *2nd Edition*

The Definitive Guide to HTML5

HTML5 Mastery

CSS Mastery *2nd Edition*

DOM Scripting *2nd Edition*

Pro .NET Best Practices

Pro Business Applications with Silverlight 5 *2nd Edition*

Pro Silverlight 5 in C# *4 Edition*

Pro Silverlight 5 in VB *4 Edition*

Beginning Kinect Programming with the Microsoft Kinect SDK

Meet the Kinect

Hacking the Kinect

Pro Visual Studio LightSwitch 2011 Development

Pro NuGet

Beginning Windows Phone App Development

Pro ASP.NET MVC 3 Framework *3rd Edition*

Pro LINQ

Pro .NET 4 Parallel Programming in C#

About the Author

 **Adam Freeman** is an experienced IT professional who has held senior positions in a range of companies, most recently serving as chief technology officer and chief operating officer of a global bank. Now retired, he spends his time writing and running.

His other upcoming publications include:

Available in May.

Metro Revealed: Building Windows 8 apps with XAML and C#

Available this summer.

Pro JavaScript for Web Apps

Available this fall.

Pro Windows 8 Development with HTML5 and JavaScript
Pro Visual Studio 11
Pro ASP.NET MVC 4 *4 Edition.*
Pro ASP.NET 4.5 in C# *5th Edition*
Pro ASP.NET 4.5 in VB *5th Edition*

His other publications include:

The Definitive Guide to HTML5
Applied ASP.NET 4 in Context
Pro ASP.NET MVC 3 Framework *3rd Edition*
Pro jQuery
Introducing Visual C# 2010
Pro ASP.NET 4 in C# 2010 *4 Edition*
Pro ASP.NET 4 in VB 2010 *3rd Edition*
Pro LINQ
Pro .NET 4 Parallel Programming in C#
Visual C# 2010 Recipes

About the Technical Reviewer

Fabio Claudio Ferracchiati is a senior consultant and a senior analyst/developer using Microsoft technologies. He works for Brain Force (http://www.brainforce.com) in its Italian branch (http://www.brainforce.it). He is a Microsoft Certified Solution Developer for .NET, a Microsoft Certified Application Developer for .NET, a Microsoft Certified Professional, and a prolific author and technical reviewer. Over the past ten years, he's written articles for Italian and international magazines and coauthored more than ten books on a variety of computer topics.

Acknowledgments

I would like to thank everyone at Apress for working so hard to bring this book to print. In particular, I would like to thank Jennifer Blackwell for keeping me on track and Ewan Buckingham for commissioning and editing this revision. I would also like to thank my technical reviewer, Fabio, whose efforts made this book far better than it would have been otherwise.

Getting Started

Metro apps are an important addition to Microsoft Windows 8, providing the cornerstone for a single, consistent programming and interaction model across desktops, tablets, and smartphones. The Metro app user experience is very different from previous generations of Windows applications: Metro apps are full-screen and favor a usability style that is simple, direct, and free from distractions.

Metro apps represent a complete departure from previous versions of Windows. There are entirely new APIs, new interaction controls, and a very different approach to managing the life cycle of applications.

Metro apps can be developed using a range of languages, including C#, Visual Basic, C++, and, the topic of this book, JavaScript. Windows 8 is the first version of Windows that embraces the skills and knowledge of web application developers and makes JavaScript and HTML first-class citizens in application development.

In this book, I show you how you can build on your knowledge of web app development to create Metro apps using HTML and JavaScript. The result is apps that look and feel like an integral part of the Windows experience and that take advantage of core platform facilities.

This book gives you an essential jump start into the world of Metro; by the end, you will understand how to use the controls and features that define the core Metro experience.

About This Book

This book is for experienced HTML and JavaScript developers who want to get a head start creating Metro applications for Windows 8 using the Consumer Preview test release. I explain the concepts and techniques you need to get up to speed quickly and to boost your Metro development techniques and knowledge before the final version of Windows 8 is released.

What Do You Need to Know Before You Read This Book?

You need to have a good understanding of HTML and JavaScript, ideally from creating rich web apps. You need to understand the DOM API, know how events work, and have a solid grasp of the HTML elements and their DOM object counterparts.

Do You Need to Know About HTML5?

No. You can use some of the HTML5 JavaScript APIs when developing Metro apps, but that is not the focus of this book. A good basic knowledge of HTML4 or HTML5 will be enough, combined with solid JavaScript experience.

What Software Do You Need for This Book?

You will need the Windows 8 Consumer Preview and the Visual Studio 11 Express Beta for Windows 8. You can download both of them from `http://preview.windows.com`. You don't need any other tools to develop Metro applications or for the examples in this book.

Windows 8 Consumer Preview is not a finished product, and it has some stability issues. You'll get the best experience if you install Windows 8 directly onto a well-specified PC, but you can get by with a virtual machine if you are not ready to make the switch.

What Is the Structure of This Book?

I focus on the key techniques and features that make a Metro app. You already know how to write HTML and use form elements to gather input from the user, and I am not going to waste your time teaching you what you already know. This book is about translating your web app development experience into the Metro world, and that means focusing on what makes a Metro app special.

I have taken a relaxed approach to mixing topics. Aside from the main theme in each chapter, you'll find some essential context to explain why features are important and why you should implement them. Along the way, I'll show you the conventions for writing JavaScript Metro apps and introduce as many Metro features as I can. By the end of this book, you will understand how to build a Metro app that integrates properly into Windows 8 and presents a user experience that is consistent with Metro apps written using other technologies, such as XAML/C#.

This is a primer to get you started on Metro programming for Windows 8. It isn't a comprehensive tutorial; as a consequence, I have focused on those topics that are the major building blocks for a Metro app. There is a lot of information that I just couldn't fit into such a slim volume. If you do want more comprehensive coverage of Metro development, then Apress will be publishing my *Pro Windows 8 Development with HTML5 and JavaScript* book for the final release of Windows 8.

The following sections summarize the chapters in this book.

Chapter 1: Getting Started

Aside from introducing this book, I show you how to create the Visual Studio project for the example Metro app that I use throughout this book. I show you how to use the JavaScript tools in Visual Studio, how to test your Metro apps in the Visual Studio simulator, and how to use the debugger.

Chapter 2: Data and Bindings

Data is at the heart of any Metro application, and in this chapter I show you how to define a view model and how to use Metro data bindings to bring that data into your application layouts. These techniques are essential to building Metro apps that are easy to extend, easy to test, and easy to maintain. Along the way, I'll show you how to define Metro JavaScript namespaces, create observable arrays, use JavaScript promises, and generate content using templates.

Chapter 3: Application Controls

Certain user interface controls are common to all Metro apps, regardless of which language is used to create them. In this chapter, I show you how to create and configure AppBars and Flyouts, which are the two most important of these common controls; together they form the backbone of your interaction with the user. I also show you how to break up your Metro content and code into pieces to make your app easy to manage and how to bring those pieces together at runtime.

Chapter 4: Layouts and Tiles

The functionality of a Metro application extends to the Windows 8 Start menu, which offers a number of ways to present the user with additional information. In this chapter, I show you how to create and update dynamic Start tiles and how to apply badges to those tiles.

I also show you how to deal with the Metro *snapped* and *filled* layouts, which allow a Windows 8 user to use two Metro apps side by side. You can adapt to these layouts using CSS or JavaScript, and I show you both approaches.

Chapter 5: Life-cycle Events

Windows applies a very specific life-cycle model to Metro apps. In this chapter, I explain how the model works, show you how to receive and respond to critical life-cycle events, and describe how to manage the transitions between suspended and running applications. I demonstrate how to create and manage asynchronous tasks and how to bring them under control when your application is suspended. Finally, I show you how to support Metro *contracts*, which allow your application to seamlessly integrate into the wider Windows 8 experience.

Tell Me More About the Example Metro Application

The example application for this book is a simple grocery list manager called *MetroGrocer*. As an application in its own right, MetroGrocer is pretty dull, but it is a perfect platform to demonstrate the most important Metro features. You can see how the app looks by the end of this book in Figure 1-1.

This is a book about programming and not design. MetroGrocer is not a pretty application, and I don't even implement all of its features. It is a vehicle for demonstrating coding techniques, pure and simple. You have picked up the wrong book if you want to learn about design. If you want to do some heavy-duty Metro programming, then you are in the right place.

Is There a Lot of Code in This Book?

Yes. In fact, there is so much code that I couldn't fit it all in without some editing. So, when I introduce a new topic or make a lot of changes, I'll show you a complete HTML or JavaScript file. When I make small changes or want to emphasize a few critical lines of code or markup, I'll show you a code fragment, like the one in Listing 1-1, which is taken from Chapter 5.

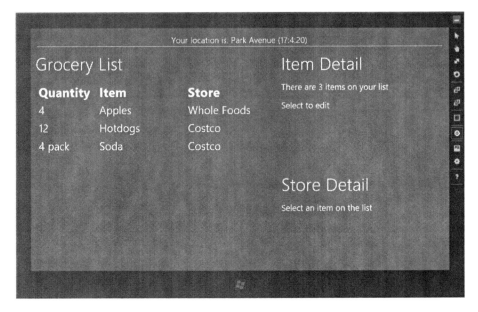

Figure 1-1. *The example application*

Listing 1-1. *A Code Fragment*

```
...
if (e.kind == actNS.ActivationKind.search) {
    Search.searchAndSelect(e.queryText);
}
...
```

These fragments make it easier for me to pack more code into the book, but they make following along with the examples in isolation by typing them into Visual Studio more difficult. If you do want to follow the examples, then the best way is to download the source code for this book from Apress.com. The code is available for free and includes a complete Visual Studio project for every chapter in the book, which means you'll always be able to see the big picture.

I have focused on introducing new techniques and avoid showing you what you already know. A causality of this approach is CSS style sheets. CSS classes are very repetitive and verbose, and I don't want to waste time by listing endless reams of styles when I could be showing you something more interesting. You can find all of the CSS in the source code download if you want to make your projects look identical to the example project.

Getting Up and Running

In this section, I will create the project for the example Metro application that I will build up throughout the book. The application is a simple grocery list tracker; it's a tool that is simple enough to complete in this short book but that has enough features to demonstrate the most important aspects of Metro-style development.

Note   Microsoft uses the terms *Metro style* and *Metro-style app*. I can't bring myself to use these awkward terms, so I am just going to refer to *Metro* and *Metro apps*. I'll leave you to mentally insert *style* as needed.

Creating the Project

To create the example project, start Visual Studio 11 and select New Project, either from the File menu or from the link on the start page. In the New Project dialog, navigate to Installed ➤ Templates ➤ JavaScript ➤ Windows Metro style. Select the Blank Application template, set the name of the project to be MetroGrocer, and click the OK button to create the project, as shown in Figure 1-2. If this is the first time that you have used Visual Studio, then you will be prompted to obtain a developer license and perform some other initial configuration steps.

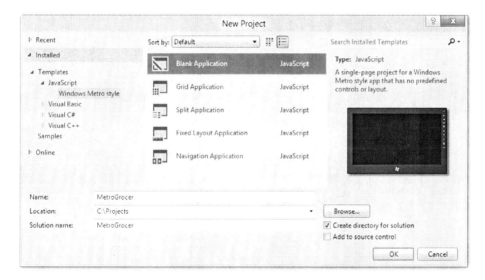

Figure 1-2. *Creating the example project*

Tip   Visual Studio includes templates preconfigured for some basic project scenarios. They are not much use, and, to my mind at least, they direct the programmer down a path that doesn't reflect the strengths of HTML5 and JavaScript. I recommend starting with a blank project and building your app from the ground up, which is the approach I have taken in this book.

The Solution Explorer shows the contents of the project, which you can see in Figure 1-3. The References folder contains the Microsoft JavaScript and CSS files that are required for Metro development. The default.html file is the page that will be loaded when the application is started, and the css, images, and js folders contain the resources that the app will depend on.

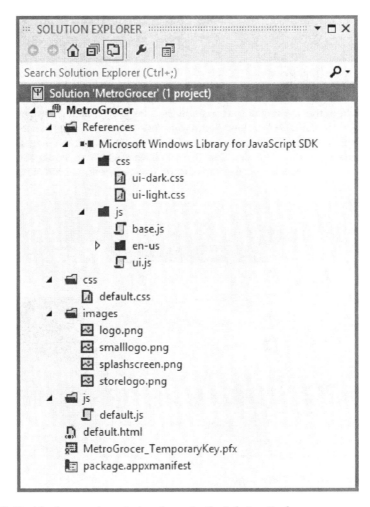

Figure 1-3. *The blank example project as shown by the Solution Explorer*

The essential files are default.html, default.css, and default.js. These files define the structure of the layout, the styles applied to it, and the code that manages the data and the interactions with the user. The fact that these files are the same ones you would generally see in web app development reflects the way in which Metro app development embraces web development techniques and tools.

In the sections that follow, I'll show you each of the most important files in the project, explain what they do, and make some initial changes to create the structure I'll need later in this book.

Exploring the default.html File

The default.html file is the one that Windows 8 loads when the Metro app is started. You can change the start file by opening the package.appxmanifest file and changing the value for the Start Page setting, but I am going to stick with the default. (Don't worry about the rest of the package.appxmanifest file; I'll come back to that in later chapters.) Metro HTML files are just like regular HTML files, and all of the HTML5 features and support available in Internet Explorer 10 is available for use in your Metro apps. Listing 1-2 shows the contents of default.html. I have highlighted the additions I made to put some basic structure in place.

Listing 1-2. *The Contents of the default.html File*

```
<!DOCTYPE html>
<html>
<head>
  <meta charset="utf-8">
  <title>MetroGrocer</title>

  <!-- WinJS references -->
  <link href="//Microsoft.WinJS.0.6/css/ui-dark.css" rel="stylesheet">
  <script src="//Microsoft.WinJS.0.6/js/base.js"></script>
  <script src="//Microsoft.WinJS.0.6/js/ui.js"></script>

  <!-- MetroGrocer references -->
  <link href="/css/default.css" rel="stylesheet">
  <script src="/js/default.js"></script>
</head>
<body>
  <div id="contentGrid">
    <div id="leftContainer" class="gridLeft">
      <h1 class="win-type-xx-large">Left Container</h1>
    </div>

    <div id="topRightContainer" class="gridRight">
      <h1 class="win-type-xx-large">Top Right Container</h1>
    </div>

    <div id="bottomRightContainer" class="gridRight">
      <h1 class="win-type-xx-large">Bottom Right Container</h1>
    </div>
  </div>
</body>
</html>
```

As the listing shows, default.html is a regular HTML5 document, but with a few key differences. For example, there are link and script elements that use nonstandard URLs:

```
<link href="//Microsoft.WinJS.0.6/css/ui-dark.css" rel="stylesheet">
<script src="//Microsoft.WinJS.0.6/js/base.js"></script>
<script src="//Microsoft.WinJS.0.6/js/ui.js"></script>
```

The base.js and ui.js files contain the JavaScript code for the *WinJS* API, which you use to create JavaScript Metro apps. I'll introduce some of the most useful parts of WinJS in later chapters.

```
THE WORLD OF METRO APIS
```

You have access to several different APIs when writing Metro apps. There is the Windows API, which is shared across all Metro apps, regardless of the language used to write them. There is the WinJS API, which is just for JavaScript Metro apps and which acts as a bridge between the capabilities of HTML/JavaScript and Windows. Finally, you have the standard Document Object Model API, which you can use to navigate the HTML markup in your application, register event handlers, and so on. JavaScript is a first-class citizen in the Metro world, and your web app development knowledge will be very useful as you start your development projects.

For the most part, the WinJS API is where you will spend most of your development time, and this is my focus for the first part of this book. The Windows API comes into its own when you want to integrate your app into the wider Windows 8 platform, which I describe in Chapters 4 and 5.

The `ui-dark.css` file contains the styles that Windows 8 uses for Metro applications, tailored for use with a dark color scheme (meaning white text on a dark background). There is a corresponding file called `ui-light.css` that you can use if you want to have dark text on a light background instead. The CSS files provide styles for all of the common HTML elements so that they fit into the Metro visual theme and are consistent with Metro apps written in other languages, such as C#/XAML. You can customize these styles by overriding them in your application, but for the most part, it is important to retain consistency with other Metro apps.

Tip It is worth opening and reading these files. One of the nice things about developing Metro apps with web technologies is that you can read the source code for the WinJS library and the CSS files. You can't edit the files, but you can see what is going on and, most usefully, set breakpoints in the WinJS code when using the debugger (which I demonstrate later in this chapter).

All three of these references are added to the `default.html` file automatically when Visual Studio creates the project. Visual Studio also adds references to the `default.css` and `default.js` files. By convention, these contain the JavaScript and CSS associated with `default.html`, but you can rename or replace these files as you see fit. I will stick with the defaults to keep things simple.

My additions to `default.html` are shown in bold in the listing. I have added a `div` element whose id is `contentGrid`. This will be the container for most of the content in my example app, and it contains three other div elements: `leftContainer`, `topRightContainer`, and `bottomRightContainer`. I'll add content to these elements as we proceed through the book.

Class names that begin with `win-type` are defined in `ui-dark.css` and are used to set the size of text in a Metro application. There are a series of styles that relate to gradations in text size from largest to smallest: `win-type-xx-large`, `win-type-x-large`, `win-type-large`, `win-type-medium`, `win-type-small`, and `win-type-x-small`. There are two other win-type styles: `win-type-ellipsis` uses an ellipsis (…) when text doesn't fit into its parent element, and `win-type-interactive` makes an element resemble a link. In `default.html`, I have used the `win-type-xx-large` style to create placeholder headers in the layout.

Exploring the default.css File

Listing 1-3 shows the contents of the default.css file. Metro projects rely on standard CSS with some vendor-specific prefixes. Microsoft used to be terrible for introducing its own CSS properties, but the ones you'll encounter in this book exist either because the relevant W3C standard is still unfinished or because there are properties that are specific to Windows 8 functionality that need to be expressed to Metro apps. You can see examples of both in the listing. The file that Visual Studio creates is very simple, and my additions are shown in bold.

Listing 1-3. *The Contents of the default.css File*

```css
body {
    background-color: #3E790A;
}

#contentGrid {
    display: -ms-grid;
    -ms-grid-rows: 1fr 1fr;
    -ms-grid-columns: 60% 60%;
    height: 100%;
    overflow: scroll;
}

#contentGrid div.gridLeft {
    margin-left: 1em;
    margin-right: 1em;
}

#contentGrid div.gridRight {
    margin-right: 1em;
}

#leftContainer {
    -ms-grid-column: 1;
    -ms-grid-row: 1;
    -ms-grid-row-span: 2;
}

#topRightContainer {
    -ms-grid-column: 2;
    -ms-grid-row: 1;
}

#bottomRightContainer {
    -ms-grid-column: 2;
    -ms-grid-row: 2;
}

@media screen and (-ms-view-state: fullscreen-landscape) {
}

@media screen and (-ms-view-state: filled) {
}
```

```
@media screen and (-ms-view-state: snapped) {
}

@media screen and (-ms-view-state: fullscreen-portrait) {
}
```

The @media rules work like regular media queries, but the property that they are responding to is specific to Metro and represents different orientations and usage scenarios (which I will explain and demonstrate in Chapter 4).

Tip Visual Studio indents CSS styles to create a visual hierarchy. This drives me crazy for some reason, so I have disabled this feature for all of the listings in this book. You can change the way that Visual Studio displays CSS by selecting Options from the Tools menu, navigating to Text Editor ➤ CSS ➤ Formatting, and unchecking the "Hierarchical indentation" option.

With my additions, I have defined a background color for the app, following the apparent Metro trend toward muted colors. The other additions I have made apply a CSS3 grid layout to the div elements I defined in default.html. You can use any of the new CSS3 layout models in a Metro app (or any CSS layout for that matter), but the specification for the grid layout has yet to be finalized, so I have to prefix my layout properties with -ms.

A QUICK INTRODUCTION TO CSS3 GRID LAYOUTS

You may not have used the grid layout because it is not consistently implemented in mainstream web browsers. Fortunately, when developing Metro web apps, we need to worry only about Internet Explorer 10, which is used to display JavaScript Metro apps to the user. In this sidebar, I provide you with a very quick introduction to the basic features of CSS3 grid layouts. To get started with a grid layout, you must set the display property and specify the number of rows and columns for the element that will contain the grid, like this:

```
#contentGrid {
   display: -ms-grid;
   -ms-grid-rows: 1fr 1fr;
   -ms-grid-columns: 60% 60%;
}
```

The display property must be set to –ms-grid. The –ms-grid-rows and –ms-grid-columns properties specify the dimensions of the grid. These can be specified as fractional units (expressed as fr), as a percentage of the available space, or as using fixed dimensions. I have specified two equal-sized rows and two columns, the width of which is set to be 60 percent of the width of the parent element.

It is common in Metro apps (or at least common in the ones developed so far) to provide a content area that is wider than the screen and allow the user to scroll from left to right to access different regions of the app. Setting the cumulative width to 120 percent sets up that behavior, which you will be able to see when I run the example web app later in this chapter.

For individual items, you specify which row and column they should appear in, like this:

```
#leftContainer {
  -ms-grid-column: 1;
  -ms-grid-row: 1;
  -ms-grid-row-span: 2;
}
```

The -ms-grid-column and -ms-grid-row properties locate an element in the grid. Both properties are 1-based, meaning that locating an element in column 1 and row 1 will place it in the top-left position in the grid. By default, elements occupy one grid square, but you can change this using the -ms-grid-row-span and -ms-grid-column-span properties. In the example, I have made the leftContainer element span two rows. The only other property of interest is -ms-grid-column-align, which I have not used in my example. This property specifies the alignment of an element within a grid square and can be set to start, end center, or stretch. If you are using a left-to-right language such as English, the start and end values left- and right-justify the element. The center value centers the element, and the stretch value resizes the element so that it completely fills its allocated space. You can create some very complex layouts using the grid properties. See the full specification at www.w3.org/TR/css3-grid for details, bearing in mind that this is not yet a ratified standard.

Exploring the default.js File

The last of the important files that Visual Studio has created is default.js, which is referenced in default.html using a standard script element. You can see the content of this file in Listing 1-4.

Listing 1-4. The Content of the default.js File

```
// For an introduction to the Blank template, see the following documentation:
// http://go.microsoft.com/fwlink/?LinkId=232509
(function () {
  "use strict";

  var app = WinJS.Application;

  app.onactivated = function (eventObject) {
    if (eventObject.detail.kind ===
        Windows.ApplicationModel.Activation.ActivationKind.launch) {

      if (eventObject.detail.previousExecutionState !==
        Windows.ApplicationModel.Activation.ApplicationExecutionState.terminated) {
        // TODO: This application has been newly launched. Initialize
        // your application here.
      } else {
```

```
            // TODO: This application has been reactivated from suspension.
            // Restore application state here.
        }
        WinJS.UI.processAll();
    }
};

app.oncheckpoint = function (eventObject) {
    // TODO: This application is about to be suspended. Save any state
    // that needs to persist across suspensions here. You might use the
    // WinJS.Application.sessionState object, which is automatically
    // saved and restored across suspension. If you need to complete an
    // asynchronous operation before your application is suspended, call
    // eventObject.setPromise().
};

app.start();
})();
```

I have not made any changes to this file aside from reformatting the code so that it fits on the page. This is where Metro apps depart from the standard web app environment and we start to see some of the Windows API poke through. Metro apps have a life cycle that is more complex than a web app, and the code added to default.js by Visual Studio provides some basic support for handling different application states. It isn't as bad as it looks, and I'll explain what you need to know about the Metro app life cycle, and how to respond to it, in Chapter 5.

USING YOUR FAVORITE JAVASCRIPT LIBRARIES WITH METRO

By this point, you will have realized that a lot of your experience in web app development is directly transferable to the world of Metro development. You can get a head start on your Metro projects by using your favorite JavaScript libraries. I am a huge fan of jQuery, for example, as anyone who has read my *Pro jQuery* book will know. For the most part, you shouldn't have any problems using well-written libraries as long as you avoid areas where Metro follows a different model than mainstream browsers. So, for example, jQuery works well in Metro apps, but be careful when using the ready event. In a Metro app, you need to respond directly to the life-cycle events. Another area to avoid is asynchronous script loading; I have had some problems in this area with the Windows 8 Consumer Preview, and it is simpler just to load your code using a regular script element.

There are some libraries, however, that it just doesn't make much sense to use. Examples include user interface toolkits such as jQuery UI and jQuery Mobile. You can make these work in Metro, but you end up with an application that doesn't follow the distinctive Metro style and that may not respond to touch events in quite the same way as other Metro apps.

As a general guide, I recommend you get used to the capabilities of the WinJS API before you start using your favorite JavaScript packages. Microsoft has provided a reasonably solid set of foundation capabilities, including interface controls, data binding, and even a cut-down version of jQuery. These sometimes have flaws, some of which you will see in this book, but I suggest you learn what WinJS has to offer before adding other JavaScript libraries.

Starting and Debugging a JavaScript Metro App

The best way of testing and debugging a Metro app is using the simulator, which is included as part of the Visual Studio download. In the Visual Studio window, you will see a right-arrow next to the words *Local Machine*. Click the small down arrow to the right of the words, and select Simulator from the menu, as shown in Figure 1-4.

To start the Metro app, click the button, which will now read Simulator. A new window will appear that displays the Metro app, as shown in Figure 1-5.

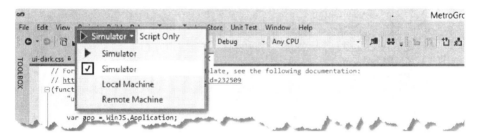

Figure 1-4. *Selecting the simulator for a Metro application*

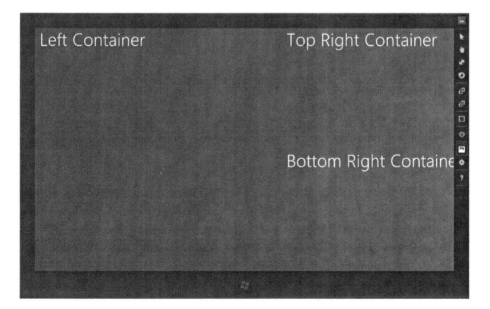

Figure 1-5. *The Metro simulator*

This is the best mechanism for testing Metro apps because it allows you to simulate device capabilities that are not natively available on your development machine. If you explore the buttons on the right edge of the simulator window, you will see options for changing the screen resolution, changing the orientation of the device, and simulating touch interactions and location data.

Note   You will recall that I set the width of the grid layout to 120 percent of the available space when I added styles to the `default.css` file earlier in this chapter. You can see the effect of this in the figure. The text for the bottom-right container is clipped, and part of the layout isn't immediately visible. You can slide the view by touch or by using the mouse.

Reloading the Metro Application

One of the nice aspects of using JavaScript to develop Metro apps is that you don't have to stop and restart the app on the simulator to reflect any changes you make. To demonstrate this, I have made a couple of simple changes. First, I have changed the text contained in one of the `div` elements in `default.html`, as shown in Listing 1-5.

Listing 1-5. *Making an HTML Change*

```
...
<div id="leftContainer" class="gridLeft">
  <h1 class="win-type-xx-large">Left Full Container</h1>
</div>
...
```

I have also made a change to `default.css`, as shown in Listing 1-6, assigning a different background color to another element.

Listing 1-6. *Making a CSS Change*

```
...
#topRightContainer {
  -ms-grid-column: 2;
  -ms-grid-row: 1;
  background-color: #808080;
}
...
```

Tip   When I show partial listings like these, only the bold area has changed. The rest of the file remains just as it was in earlier listings. I know some readers prefer that all code listings be shown complete, but I need to pack a lot of information into a slim book, and this is an excellent way of increasing the content density. Don't forget that you can get the complete source code, without charge, from Apress.com.

Figure 1-6 shows the Visual Studio controls that control the execution of the Metro app in the simulator. The first four start, pause, stop, and restart execution. These are the traditional debugger controls that Visual Studio has had for as long as I can remember.

Figure 1-6. *Controls for restarting and reloading the Metro app*

The addition is the reload button, which I have highlighted on its own and which is to the right of the other controls. Clicking this button quickly reloads the content of your Metro app and immediately reflects any changes. You can see the effect of my HTML and CSS changes in Figure 1-7.

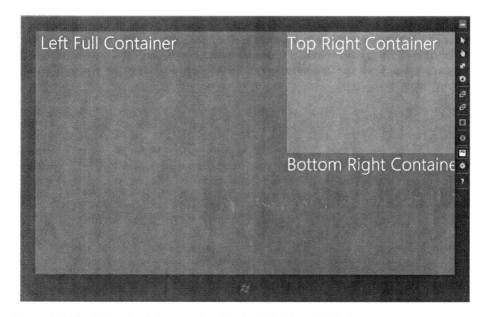

Figure 1-7. *The Metro simulator now showing the HTML5 and CSS changes*

It isn't just the HTML and CSS that are reloaded. The JavaScript for the application is refreshed as well. This is a nice and quick way of getting an iterative write-and-test development cycle going for Metro apps.

Debugging Metro Apps

Visual Studio has an excellent debugger, and it can be used very easily to track down problems in JavaScript Metro apps. In my own application code, I find it easiest to add the debugger keyword to my code. When the runtime encounters the keyword, the debugger breaks, and I can step through my code, inspect variables, and execute little snippets of code using the JavaScript console.

You can use the `debugger` keyword only for code you can modify, however, which means that I have to take a different approach when I want to break the debugger on a statement in one of the Microsoft `base.js` and `ui.js` JavaScript files. To do this, I have to select the statement I am interested in, right-click, and select Breakpoint ➤ Insert Breakpoint from the pop-up menu. The effect is the same, but no modifications are made to the file.

I recommend exploring the Visual Studio debugger; it is more sophisticated than the developer tools available in browsers, and it is well worth a couple of hours to get to grips with how it works.

Summary

In this chapter, I introduced the structure of the book and provided a brief preview of what you will find in the chapters that follow. I also showed you the anatomy of a basic Metro project and created the example project that I will build on for the rest of the book. Finally, I showed you how to use the simulator to run a Metro application and briefly touched on the two ways to cause the Visual Studio debugger to break when running your code. In the next chapter, I'll start to add some functionality to the example and begin using some of the features of the WinJS API. I start by defining a view model and demonstrating how to bind the data it contains to the Metro app layout; this is an essential technique for building robust apps that are easily to build, scale, and maintain.

Data and Bindings

In this chapter, I show you how to define and use the data that forms the core of a Metro application. To do this, I will be loosely following the *view model* pattern, which allows me to cleanly separate the data from the HTML that is used to present it to the user. This makes applications easier to write, test, and maintain.

You may already be familiar with models and view models from design patterns such as Model-View-Controller (MVC) and Model-View-View Controller (MVVC). I am not going to get into the details of these patterns in this book. There is a lot of good information about MVC and MVVC available, starting with Wikipedia, which has some very balanced and insightful descriptions.

I find the benefits of using a view model to be enormous and well worth considering for all but the simplest Metro projects, and I recommend you seriously consider following the same path. I am not a pattern zealot, and I firmly believe in taking the parts of patterns and techniques that solve real problems and adapting them to work in specific projects. To that end, you will find that I take a pretty liberal view of how a view model should be used.

This chapter is largely focused on the behind-the-scenes plumbing in a Metro app. I start slowly, showing you the conventions for adding JavaScript code to a Metro project and how to use the Metro JavaScript features to reduce global namespace pollution. From there, I define a simple view model and demonstrate different techniques for bringing the data from the view model into the application display. This chapter is all about creating a solid foundation for a Metro app and getting to grips with the core Metro JavaScript functionality. Table 2-1 provides the summary for this chapter.

Creating the JavaScript File

The first step is to create a new JavaScript file. Unlike a web app, there is no reason to reduce the number of JavaScript files in a Metro application because they are already resident on the user's computer when the application is started. This means I don't have to concatenate files or worry about minimizing code to reduce the size of script files. Instead, I can create separate files for each main application feature.

Add a new file by right-clicking the js folder in the Solution Explorer window and selecting Add ➤ New Item from the menu. Select JavaScript File from the list, set the name to viewmodel.js, and click the Add button to create the file. Visual Studio will add a new empty file to the project and open it for editing. Add the statements shown in Listing 2-1.

Table 2-1. *Chapter Summary*

Problem	Solution	Listing
Create a view model.	Use the WinJS.Namespace.define method to create a global object containing your application data.	1
Display values from the view model.	Use the data-win-bind attribute to create declarative bindings and call the WinJS.Binding.processAll method to process them.	2, 3
Create a dynamic binding.	Use the WinJS.Binding.as method to create an observable data property. Assign new values to the property to trigger updates in the HTML.	4, 6, 7
Create an observable data properties in a globally available namespace object.	Ensure that the object with the observable properties isn't directly exported by the WinJS.Namespace.define method.	5
Create observable arrays.	Use the WinJS.Binding.List object.	8, 9, 10
Generate HTML elements from observable arrays.	User the WinJS template feature.	11, 12

Listing 2-1. *The Initial Contents of the View Model Class*

```
/// <reference path="//Microsoft.WinJS.0.6/js/base.js" />
/// <reference path="//Microsoft.WinJS.0.6/js/ui.js" />
(function () {
  "use strict";

  WinJS.Namespace.define("ViewModel.UserData", {
    // private members
    _shoppingItems: [],
    _preferredStores: [],

    // public members
    homeZipCode: null,

    getStores: function () {
      return this._preferredStores;
    },

    addStore: function(newStore) {
      this._preferredStores.push(newStore);
    },

    getItems: function () {
      return this._shoppingItems;
    },

    addItem: function(newName, newQuantity, newStore) {
      this._shoppingItems.push({
        item: newName,
```

```
          quantity: newQuantity,
          store: newStore
      });
    }
  });

  ViewModel.UserData.homeZipCode = "NY 10118";

  ViewModel.UserData.addStore("Whole Foods");
  ViewModel.UserData.addStore("Kroger");
  ViewModel.UserData.addStore("Costco");
  ViewModel.UserData.addStore("Walmart");

  ViewModel.UserData.addItem("Apples", 4, "Whole Foods");
  ViewModel.UserData.addItem("Hotdogs", 12, "Costco");
  ViewModel.UserData.addItem("Soda", "4 pack", "Costco");

})();
```

I'll return to the view model in a moment, but first I need to explain some of the other parts of the code and the conventions they represent. I won't do this for subsequent files, but there is some useful context to put in place as you get started with Metro development.

Using Code Completion

Visual Studio supports JavaScript code completion in the editor, which makes writing code simpler and less error-prone. You must use a `reference` element to bring JavaScript files into scope for code completion for files that are not in the local directory, like this:

```
/// <reference path="//Microsoft.WinJS.0.6/js/base.js" />
/// <reference path="//Microsoft.WinJS.0.6/js/ui.js" />
```

Prefixing the `reference` element with three slash (/) characters brings the reference to the attention of Visual Studio and causes the JavaScript runtime to treat the statement like a comment. With these additions, code-competition support for the WinJS API is added to the `view-model.js` file. You need to add these reference elements to each of your JavaScript files if you want WinJS completion.

Tip JavaScript code completion in the Visual Studio 11 beta is a little unreliable. I find that trying to complete code often causes Visual Studio to crash—so much so that I have taken to disabling code completion for JavaScript files in the Visual Studio options.

Reducing Global Namespace Pollution

One of the biggest problems in JavaScript is variable name collision. JavaScript variables defined outside a function are globally available, and since there are only so many meaningful variable names, it is only a matter of time before two different regions of code try to use the same variable name for different purposes. Global variables are said to be part of the *global namespace*, and defining global variables is often described as *polluting the global namespace*.

Metro JavaScript files follow three different conventions to reduce namespace pollution, all of which you should adopt.

Creating Namespaces

The WinJS API helps reduce global namespace pollution through the define method of the Namespace object:

```
WinJS.Namespace.define("ViewModel.UserData", {
    // ... members for the ViewModel.UserData object are defined here ...
});
```

The first argument to the define method is the global name that you want to assign to your object. In this case, I have specified ViewModel.UserData, which creates a global variable called ViewModel that has a UserData property. The value of the UserData property is the object that I pass as the second argument to the define method, effectively exporting the members of the object so that they are available globally via ViewModel.UserData. You'll see how this works when I come to apply the data to markup shortly.

There are a couple of reasons to use the define method, as opposed to handling this yourself. First, the ViewModel object will be created only if it doesn't already exist. This means I can easily build up the capabilities of my view model through multiple calls to the define method. The idea is that I can associate complex objects and functions together under a single global namespace object and reduce the likelihood of a variable name collision.

Tip There is a more sophisticated approach to dealing with this issue, known as the *Asynchronous Module Definition* (AMD). The AMD technique effectively eliminates global variable name collisions by allowing the consumer of a JavaScript file to pick the name of the variable through which a JavaScript library is accessed. Metro doesn't support AMD modules directly, but you can use an AMD-aware script loader such as require.js.

The second reason to use the define method is because it doesn't export any property that begins with an underscore character, which is a common JavaScript convention for defining private members. This means that when I export my UserData object, the _shoppingItems and _preferredStores properties are not globally available. This is a nice trick, and it means that the private implementation details of your global objects remain private, but, as you'll learn, it does cause some mild issues with other WinJS features.

Using Self-executing Functions

The second convention is to use self-executing functions in your JavaScript files. The basic shape of a self-executing function looks like this:

```
(function() {
    // ... statements go here ...
})();
```

Wrapping a function in parentheses and then adding another pair of parentheses immediately afterward causes the function to be defined and then executed right away. Any variables you define inside the function are scoped to the function itself and don't pollute the global namespace. When the function has been executed, the JavaScript runtime automatically cleans up any variables that have not been exported globally.

Using Strict Mode

The "use strict" statement applies some constraints on the way you can use JavaScript. One constraint is that it becomes an error to implicitly create a global variable in a function. You implicitly create a global variable when you don't use the var keyword:

```
var color1 = "blue"; // OK - scope is local to function
color2 = "red";      // Not OK - this is a global variable
```

The JavaScript runtime will generate an error if you define a variable that is implicitly global. Using strict mode is entirely optional, but it is good practice, and it disables some of the more dangerous and odd JavaScript behaviors. You can get full details of the changes that strict mode enforces by reading Appendix C of the ECMAScript Language Specification at www.ecma-international.org/publications/files/ECMA-ST/Ecma-262.pdf.

Returning to the View Model

Now that I have explained the context and conventions of a Metro JavaScript file, I can turn to the definition of the view model. The view model for the example Metro application will be simple, and this part of it, represented by the ViewModel.UserData object, will contain the data that is specific to the user: the user's home zip code, their grocery list, and the stores from which they buy groceries.

I defined two arrays that will hold details of the items on the shopping list and the user's preferred stores, _shoppingItems and _preferredStores. These properties are not exported as part of the ViewModel.UserData object because they start with an underscore. To provide access to the data, I have defined a set of functions that return the array data and that accept new items to be added to the arrays. The homeZipCode property *is* public and forms part of the globally available ViewModel.UserData object. You can read and change the value of this property directly.

Note   The shape and structure of the UserData object are a little odd because I want to show different aspects of the WinJS API. In a real project, you would treat the data items in a more consistent manner.

So that there is some data to work with in the application, I have added some statements to the self-executing function to define a zip code, add some stores, and put a few simple items on the shopping list:

```
ViewModel.UserData.homeZipCode = "NY 10118";

ViewModel.UserData.addStore("Whole Foods");
ViewModel.UserData.addStore("Kroger");
```

```
ViewModel.UserData.addStore("Costco");
ViewModel.UserData.addStore("Walmart");

ViewModel.UserData.addItem("Apples", 4, "Whole Foods");
ViewModel.UserData.addItem("Hotdogs", 12, "Costco");
ViewModel.UserData.addItem("Soda", "4 pack", "Costco");
```

Using Data Binding

Data binding is the mechanism by which you include data from your view model in the HTML that is displayed to the user. The WinJS API supports binding through the WinJS.Binding namespace. Data binding is the key to being able to use a view model in a Metro app. I recommend investing time to learn how to use the WinJS binding capabilities fully if you want to build scalable and robust Metro applications.

Tip WinJS data binding isn't as complete or flexible as some of the more widely used web app JavaScript libraries such as Knockout.js, Backbone, and Angular.js. You can easily use these libraries in your Metro app, but my recommendation is to take the time to understand the WinJS alternative and see how the functionality evolves as the final version of Windows 8 approaches.

Using Basic Declarative Bindings

The simplest way to use bindings is *declaratively,* meaning that you include details of the view model data directly in your HTML markup. Listing 2-2 shows how I can bind to the homeZipCode value in default.html.

Listing 2-2. *A Simple Declarative Binding*

```
<!DOCTYPE html>
<html>
<head>
  <meta charset="utf-8">
  <title>MetroGrocer</title>

  <!-- WinJS references -->
  <link href="//Microsoft.WinJS.0.6/css/ui-dark.css" rel="stylesheet">
  <script src="//Microsoft.WinJS.0.6/js/base.js"></script>
  <script src="//Microsoft.WinJS.0.6/js/ui.js"></script>

  <!-- MetroGrocer references -->
  <link href="/css/default.css" rel="stylesheet">
  <script src="/js/viewmodel.js"></script>
  <script src="/js/default.js"></script>
</head>
<body>
  <div id="contentGrid">
    <div id="leftContainer" class="gridLeft">
```

```
      <h1 class="win-type-xx-large">Left Full Container</h1>
      <div class="win-type-x-large">
        The zip code is:
        <span data-win-bind="innerText: UserData.homeZipCode"></span>
      </div>
    </div>

    <div id="topRightContainer" class="gridRight">
      <h1 class="win-type-xx-large">Top Right Container</h1>
    </div>

    <div id="bottomRightContainer" class="gridRight">
      <h1 class="win-type-xx-large">Bottom Right Container</h1>
    </div>
  </div>
</body>
</html>
```

I have added a script element that adds viewmodel.js to the HTML document. The most important addition, however, is the span element and its data-win-bind attribute.

 Tip The order of script elements is important in a Metro app, just like it is in a web app. The code in my default.js file will depend on my view model, so I must ensure that the script element for viewmodel.js appears before the one for default.js.

There are two parts to a declarative binding. The first part is the name of a property defined by the HTMLElement object that represents the element in the Document Object Model (DOM). I have used innerText, which will set the text content of the span element. The property name is followed by a colon (:) and then the name of the data item that should be assigned to that property. I have specified UserData.homeZipCode.

 Tip Declarative bindings will silently fail if you specify any property name that is also a reserved JavaScript keyword. This means, for example, that you avoid using the class property in bindings and use the className property instead.

It isn't enough just to add data-win-binding attributes to HTML elements. I also have to tell the WinJS API to search through the document so that the binding attributes are found and processed. Listing 2-3 shows the default.js file. I removed some of the comments that Visual Studio creates and defined some placeholder functions that I'll build on later.

Listing 2-3. *Processing WinJS Bindings*

```
(function () {

  "use strict";
```

```
var app = WinJS.Application;
app.onactivated = function (eventObject) {
  if (eventObject.detail.kind ===
     Windows.ApplicationModel.Activation.ActivationKind.launch) {

     if (eventObject.detail.previousExecutionState !==
      Windows.ApplicationModel.Activation.ApplicationExecutionState.terminated) {
         performInitialSetup(eventObject);
     } else {
         performRestore(eventObject);
     }
     WinJS.UI.processAll();
  }
};

app.oncheckpoint = function (eventObject) {
  performSuspend(eventObject);
};
app.start();

function performInitialSetup(e) {
  WinJS.Binding.processAll(document.body, ViewModel);
}

function performRestore(e) {
  // TODO
}

function performSuspend(e) {
  // TODO

}
})();
```

The import change is the call to the WinJS.Binding.processAll method. The arguments are the element from which the processing should start and the source of data values for the declarative bindings. By specifying the document.body element, I have told WinJS to process the entire document. The second argument tells WinJS to use the ViewModel object as the data source.

Declarative data bindings are relative to the data source, which is why the binding in my example references UserData.homeZipCode and not ViewModel.UserData.homeZipCode:

```
<span data-win-bind="innerText: UserData.homeZipCode"></span>
```

The result of these changes is that the content of the span element is set to the value of the homeZipCode property, as shown in Figure 2-1.

Figure 2-1. *Using a declarative binding to display view model values*

Creating Dynamic Bindings

The binding that I used in the previous example is *static*, meaning that there is no ongoing relationship between the value of the view model property and the value of the span element that contains the binding declaration. Static bindings are like a snapshot of a view model value. Once the snapshot has been taken, the value in the markup is fixed, even if the value of the property changes.

Dynamic bindings, where property changes *do* result in updated elements, are more useful for most applications. In WinJS, declarative bindings are automatically dynamic when the data property they depend on is *observable*. To create an observable property, I have to use the WinJS.Binding.as method in my view model, as Listing 2-4 shows.

Listing 2-4. *Creating an Observable Item in the View Model*

```
/// <reference path="//Microsoft.WinJS.0.6/js/base.js" />
/// <reference path="//Microsoft.WinJS.0.6/js/ui.js" />
(function () {
  "use strict";

  WinJS.Namespace.define("ViewModel", {
    UserData: WinJS.Binding.as({

      // private members
      _shoppingItems: [],
      _preferredStores: [],
      // public members
      homeZipCode: null,

      getStores: function () {
        return this._preferredStores;
      },

      addStore: function (newStore) {
        this._preferredStores.push(newStore);
      },

      getItems: function () {
        return this._shoppingItems;
      },

      addItem: function (newName, newQuantity, newStore) {
        this._shoppingItems.push({
          item: newName,
          quantity: newQuantity,
          store: newStore
        });
      }
    })
  });

  ViewModel.UserData.homeZipCode = "NY 10118";

  ViewModel.UserData.addStore("Whole Foods");
```

```
ViewModel.UserData.addStore("Kroger");
ViewModel.UserData.addStore("Costco");
ViewModel.UserData.addStore("Walmart");

ViewModel.UserData.addItem("Apples", 4, "Whole Foods");
ViewModel.UserData.addItem("Hotdogs", 12, "Costco");
ViewModel.UserData.addItem("Soda", "4 pack", "Costco");
})();
```

The change here is subtle but important. The WinJS.Binding.as takes an object as its argument and returns an object whose *simple properties* are observable. A simple property is one where the value is primitive, such as a number or a string. Properties whose values are objects, arrays, or functions are not simple and are not made observable by the as method.

The WinJS.Binding.as method replaces data properties with getters and setters that trigger notifications when the property value change. Properties that refer to objects, arrays, or functions are left unchanged by the as method. (I explain how to handle arrays later in this chapter.)

You *must* call the as method on objects, rather than on properties or simple values. If you call WinJS.Binding.as directly on a property, you will simply get back the property value, and any bindings that use the property won't automatically update:

```
// this will NOT update
var myObject = {
  myObservableValue: WinJS.Binding.as("MyInitialValue")
};

// this WILL update
var myOtherObject = WinJS.Binding.as({
  myObservableValue: "MyInitialValue"
});
```

No error is reported when you try to create an observable value using the first approach. WinJS just quietly ignores the request, and you get a static binding. Following the second technique will allow you to create bindings that update when the value changes.

Combining Namespaces with Observable Items

There are occasions when the WinJS API creates the impression that different development teams could have coordinated their efforts more carefully. One such example comes when trying to create an observable data item on an object that is exported globally using the WinJS.Namespace.define method.

The WinJS.Binding.as method adds a number of private members to an object when it processes the simple properties, following the common convention of prefixing the names of these members with an underscore. But, as I explained, the WinJS.Namespace.define method won't export these members globally. To get around this conflict, I have adjusted the way that I create my ViewModel.UserData object, as Listing 2-5 shows.

Listing 2-5. *Adjusting the Structure of a Global Object to Export Private Members*

```
...
WinJS.Namespace.define("ViewModel", {
  UserData: WinJS.Binding.as({
```

```
    // ... members for UserData object go here...
  })
});
...
```

The define method doesn't remove the private members of properties within the object it exports, which allows me to export the private members of my UserData object by specifying it as a property of the ViewModel object.

Updating an Observable Data Item

Updates from observable data items flow in only one direction, from the view model to the binding. You must use conventional JavaScript DOM API techniques to make data updates flow in the other direction, from the elements to the view model. Listing 2-6 shows the addition of input and button elements to the markup in default.html for updating the homeZipCode property.

Listing 2-6. *Capturing Data That Will Be Used to Update the View Model*

```
<!DOCTYPE html>
<html>
<head>
  <meta charset="utf-8">
  <title>MetroGrocer</title>
  <!-- WinJS references -->
  <link href="//Microsoft.WinJS.0.6/css/ui-dark.css" rel="stylesheet">
  <script src="//Microsoft.WinJS.0.6/js/base.js"></script>
  <script src="//Microsoft.WinJS.0.6/js/ui.js"></script>
  <!-- MetroGrocer references -->
  <link href="/css/default.css" rel="stylesheet">
  <script src="/js/viewmodel.js"></script>
  <script src="/js/default.js"></script>
</head>
<body>
  <div id="contentGrid">
    <div id="leftContainer" class="gridLeft">
      <h1 class="win-type-xx-large">Left Full Container</h1>

      <div class="win-type-x-large">
        The zip code is:
        <span data-win-bind="innerText: UserData.homeZipCode"></span>
      </div>
      <div class="win-type-x-large">
        <label for="newZip">Enter new zip code:</label>
        <input id="newZip" data-win-bind="value: UserData.homeZipCode"/>
        <button id="newZipButton">Update Zip Code</button>
      </div>
    </div>

    <div id="topRightContainer" class="gridRight">
      <h1 class="win-type-xx-large">Top Right Container</h1>
    </div>
```

```
    <div id="bottomRightContainer" class="gridRight">
      <h1 class="win-type-xx-large">Bottom Right Container</h1>
    </div>
  </div>
</body>
</html>
```

No Metro-specific technique is required to take the value from the input element and update the view model value. Listing 2-7 shows the changes to the default.js file that respond to the click event from the button element and update the view model using the value property of the input element DOM object.

Listing 2-7. *Updating the View Model in Response to the Change Event*

```
...
function performInitialSetup(e) {
  WinJS.Binding.processAll(document.body, ViewModel);

  WinJS.Utilities.query('#newZipButton').listen("click", function (e) {
    ViewModel.UserData.homeZipCode=WinJS.Utilities.query('#newZip')[0].value;
  });
}
...
```

The WinJS.Utilities namespace contains subset of the functionality found in utility libraries such as jQuery. The API is broadly the same as jQuery, but instead of the $ shortcut function, querying elements is done through the WinJS.Utilities.query method. Not all of the functionality of jQuery is available, but you can use the WinJS.Utilities namespace to locate elements, apply CSS styles and classes, and set up handlers for events.

In this listing, I have used the query method to search the HTML document for the newZipButton element and called the listen method on the result to set up a handler for the click event. When the button is clicked, I locate the input element, read the value property from the object, and assign it to the homeZipCode property in the view model.

The result from the query method is an array of elements. There is no equivalent to the jQuery val method, so I treat the response like an array to get the HTMLElement object that represents the first element that matches my selector and then read the value property. The result is that the user can enter a new zip code in the input element, and when the button is clicked, the view model zip code value is updated. Since the update is applied to an observable property, the content of the span element is updated automatically to show the new value through its binding, as illustrated by Figure 2-2.

Figure 2-2. *Updating an observable value in the view model*

> **Tip**   If you have used a web app view model library such as Knockout.js, you might be
> used to updating view model values by calling methods, like this: `ViewModel.UserData.`
> `homeZipCode(myNewValue)`. Knockout uses methods to preserve compatibility with older brows-
> ers that don't support getters and setters, including most previous versions of Internet Explorer.
> Internet Explorer 10, which is used to display HTML5 Metro apps, *does* support getters and set-
> ters, which means you can assign values directly, just as I did in the example.

Creating Observable Arrays

Making arrays observable requires a little more effort. To begin with, you must use the `WinJS.`
`Binding.List` class to create a wrapper around the array you want to work with. Listing 2-8
shows the `List` class applied to my `viewmodel` in the `viewmodel.js` file.

Listing 2-8. *Using the List Class to Create Observable Arrays*

```
/// <reference path="//Microsoft.WinJS.0.6/js/base.js" />
/// <reference path="//Microsoft.WinJS.0.6/js/ui.js" />
(function () {
  "use strict";

  var shoppingItemsList = new WinJS.Binding.List();
  var preferredStoresList = new WinJS.Binding.List();

  WinJS.Namespace.define("ViewModel", {
    UserData: WinJS.Binding.as({
      homeZipCode: null,

      getStores: function () {
        return preferredStoresList;
      },

      addStore: function (newStore) {
        preferredStoresList.push(newStore);
      },

      getItems: function () {
        return shoppingItemsList;
      },

      addItem: function (newName, newQuantity, newStore) {
        shoppingItemsList.push({
          item: newName,
          quantity: newQuantity,
          store: newStore
        });
      }
    })
  });
```

```
// statements to add test data removed for brevity
})();
```

Creating a List is simple, but you will encounter problems if you try to do so within the scope of an object that has passed to the WinJS.Binding.as method (there is a clash of assumptions over the value of the special this variable). To avoid this problem, define your lists outside of the view model, as I have done in the example.

Using a List object isn't the same as using an array. The most important difference is that you cannot use array indexers to read or write data values. Instead, you must use the getAt and setAt methods. Other array members, such as push and pop, are supported by List, and there are some useful additions for sorting and projecting the contents of List objects.

Another important difference is that you cannot access array values using declarative bindings. Instead, you must set values in the DOM using JavaScript and handle events emitted by the List object to keep those values up-to-date. Listing 2-9 shows elements in the default. html file that display the number of items in one of the view model lists and some buttons to add and remove items.

Listing 2-9. *Elements for Interacting with a List Object*

```
...
<div id="leftContainer" class="gridLeft">
  <h1 class="win-type-xx-large">Left Full Container</h1>

  <div class="win-type-x-large">
    The last item is<span id="listInfo"></span>
  </div>
  <div class="win-type-x-large">
    <button id="addItemButton">Add Item</button>
    <button id="removeItemButton">Remove Item</button>
  </div>
</div>
...
```

There are no special data attributes in these elements, just regular HTML. Everything happens in the default.js file, as shown in Listing 2-10.

Listing 2-10. *Using JavaScript to Bridge Between HTML Elements and a WinJS.Binding.List*

```
...
function performInitialSetup(e) {

  WinJS.Utilities.query('button').listen("click", function (e) {
    if (this.id == "addItemButton") {
      ViewModel.UserData.addItem("Ice Cream", 1, "Vanilla", "Walmart");
    } else {
      ViewModel.UserData.getItems().pop();
    }
  });

  var setValue = function () {
    var list = ViewModel.UserData.getItems();
```

```
   document.getElementById("listInfo").innerText =
      list.getAt(list.length - 1).item;

};

var eventTypes = ["itemchanged", "iteminserted", "itemmoved", "itemremoved"];
eventTypes.forEach(function (type) {
   ViewModel.UserData.getItems().addEventListener(type, setValue);
});

setValue();
}
...
```

The List object defines four events that are triggered when the data items change. These events are itemchanged, iteminserted, itemmoved, and itemremoved. The List object defines an addEventListener method that allows for the registration of event handler functions for these events. In the listing, I register the same handler function for all four events; it updates the innerText property of the span element to display the item property of the first element in the List.

The two button elements add and remove items from the List. I have left the addItem method in the view model because I prefer to have little helper functions like this to make the structure of the data objects more consistent, but I could have directly called the push method on the List object to get the same effect. You can see the result in Figure 2-3.

Figure 2-3. *Displaying details of List objects in HTML elements*

Tip   I was able to remove the call to the WinJS.Binding.processAll method from this listing because there are no declarative bindings in the HTML document.

Using Templates

List objects come into their own when used with *binding templates*, which allow for regions of markup to be duplicated for a series of data values. Templates are defined within the HTML document and annotated with the data-win-control attribute, as shown in Listing 2-11.

Listing 2-11. *Adding a Template to the HTML Document*

```
<!DOCTYPE html>
<html>
<head>
   <meta charset="utf-8">
```

```
    <title>MetroGrocer</title>
    <!-- WinJS references -->
    <link href="//Microsoft.WinJS.0.6/css/ui-dark.css" rel="stylesheet">
    <script src="//Microsoft.WinJS.0.6/js/base.js"></script>
    <script src="//Microsoft.WinJS.0.6/js/ui.js"></script>
    <!-- MetroGrocer references -->
    <link href="/css/default.css" rel="stylesheet">
    <script src="/js/viewmodel.js"></script>
    <script src="/js/default.js"></script>
  </head>
  <body>
    <div id="contentGrid">
      <div id="leftContainer" class="gridLeft">
        <h1 class="win-type-xx-large">Grocery List</h1>

        <table id="listTable" class="type-table-header">
          <thead>
            <tr>
              <th>Quantity</th>
              <th class="itemName">Item</th>
              <th>Store</th>
            </tr>
          </thead>
          <tbody id="itemBody"></tbody>
        </table>
      </div>

      <div id="topRightContainer" class="gridRight">
        <h1 class="win-type-xx-large">Top Right Container</h1>
      </div>

      <div id="bottomRightContainer" class="gridRight">
        <h1 class="win-type-xx-large">Bottom Right Container</h1>
      </div>
    </div>

    <!-- template for grocery list items -->
    <table>
      <tbody id="itemTemplate" data-win-control="WinJS.Binding.Template">
        <tr class="groceryItem">
          <td data-win-bind="innerText: quantity"></td>
          <td data-win-bind="innerText: item"></td>
          <td data-win-bind="innerText: store"></td>
        </tr>
      </tbody>
    </table>
    <!-- end of template for grocery list items -->
  </body>
</html>
```

There are two new table elements in this document. The first one, with the id attribute of listTable, is what the user will see. This table has a header with column titles, but the tbody element is empty. This is where I will use a template to insert a row for each item in the grocery list.

The second `table` element contains the template. The template itself is defined by the `tbody` element, but it is an oddity of WinJS templates that they need to be within well-formed HTML. You can't just define the `tbody` element as a child of the body, for example, because `tbody` elements aren't allowed to be children of body elements. This means you end up with some redundant elements in the HTML document when using templates.

Using the Template

The template is denoted by a `data-win-control` value of `WinJS.Binding.Template`. This tells WinJS to process the element, look for declarative bindings, and add some special properties to the `HTMLElement` object that represents the template element in the DOM. As mentioned previously, I like to break my projects up so that there JavaScript files for each area of functionality. To that end, I have created a new JavaScript file called `ui.js`, which is shown in Listing 2-12.

Listing 2-12. Using a Template in the ui.js File

```
/// <reference path="//Microsoft.WinJS.0.6/js/base.js" />
/// <reference path="//Microsoft.WinJS.0.6/js/ui.js" />

(function () {
  "use strict";

  WinJS.Namespace.define("UI.List", {
    displayListItems: function () {

        var templateElement = document.getElementById("itemTemplate");
        var targetElement = document.getElementById("itemBody");

        WinJS.Utilities.empty(targetElement);

        var list = ViewModel.UserData.getItems();

        for (var i = 0; i < list.length; i++) {
          templateElement.winControl.render(list.getAt(i), targetElement);
        }

        WinJS.Utilities.children(targetElement).listen("click", function (e) {
          ViewModel.State.selectedItemIndex = this.rowIndex - 1;
          WinJS.Utilities.children(targetElement).removeClass("selected");
          WinJS.Utilities.addClass(this, "selected");
        });
    },

    setupListEvents: function () {
      var eventTypes = ["itemchanged", "iteminserted", "itemmoved", "itemremoved"];
      var itemsList = ViewModel.UserData.getItems();
      eventTypes.forEach(function (type) {
        itemsList.addEventListener(type, UI.List.displayListItems);
      });
    },
  });
})();
```

I have defined a UI namespace, which contains a List object with displayListItems and setupListEvents functions. In the displayListItems function, I locate the HTMLElement objects that represent the template and the target for the generated elements. I have used the document.getElementById method to locate the elements by their id attribute values.

Tip The bold statement in the listing causes an odd Visual Studio problem. Trying to use autocompletion in this file causes Visual Studio to crash. The only way to avoid this problem is to disable the autocompletion feature for JavaScript files in the Visual Studio Tools ➤ Options menu.

The WinJS.Utilities.empty method removed the children for an element, which I do so that I don't just add new rows to the table each time the function is called.

To iterate through the items in the WinJS.Binding.List object, call the winControl. render method on the template object for each one. The winControl is created by the WinJS. UI.processAll method, and it returns the Metro-specific properties created for different types of user interface controls.

The render method is added to those elements whose data-win-control attribute is WinJS.Binding.Template. The arguments to the render method are the data item to process and the target element to which the newly generated content will be added, so, by calling the render method for each item in my grocery List object, I am able to create table rows to populate my Metro app layout.

Once I have created the table rows, I use the WinJS.Utilities.children method to set up an event listener for the click events on the newly tr elements.

Finally, I set the ViewModel.State.selectedItemIndex property (which I will define shortly) to indicate which row has been selected when the click event is received, using the rowIndex property that is available for tr elements and ensuring that the selected class is applied only to the row the user has selected.

Responding to List Changes

The other function I defined in the UI namespace is setupListEvents. This function listens for each of the list events I described in the previous section and, when they are received, calls the displayListItems function.

This allows me to use my template to render the contents of the table element whenever the contents of the list change. This is a crude way of handling list changes, but it is sufficient for a simple example. The event object passed to the handler function contains details of which list element has changed, which is essential information when implementing a more elegant approach.

Tip I set up the event handlers in a separate function so that I can call displayListItems repeatedly. If I had set up the event handlers inside the displayListItems function, then a new set of handlers would be created each time the contents of the list changed.

Tracking the Selected Item

In the `displayListItems` function, I updated the value of the `ViewModel.State.selectedIte-mIndex` property to keep track of which item in the `table` element had been selected. It is now time to define this property. Listing 2-13 shows the addition to the `viewmodel.js` file.

Listing 2-13. *Defining the selectedItemIndex Property*

```
/// <reference path="//Microsoft.WinJS.0.6/js/base.js" />
/// <reference path="//Microsoft.WinJS.0.6/js/ui.js" />

(function () {
  "use strict";

  var shoppingItemsList = new WinJS.Binding.List();
  var preferredStoresList = new WinJS.Binding.List();

  WinJS.Namespace.define("ViewModel", {
    UserData: WinJS.Binding.as({
      homeZipCode: null,

      getStores: function () {
        return preferredStoresList;
      },

      addStore: function (newStore) {
        preferredStoresList.push(newStore);
      },

      getItems: function () {
        return shoppingItemsList;
      },

      addItem: function (newName, newQuantity, newStore) {
        shoppingItemsList.push({
          item: newName,
          quantity: newQuantity,
          store: newStore
        });
      }
    }),

    State: WinJS.Binding.as({
      selectedItemIndex: -1
    })

  });
  //  ...test data removed for brevity ...
})();
```

I use the >State object to differentiate between data required for the current state of the app and data created by the user (which is represented by the UserData object).

Applying the Template to the App

Before you use a template, you must ensure that the `WinJS.UI.processAll` method has been called. This method processes the HTML document, looking for elements that have the data-win-control attribute and configuring their capabilities. This includes finding and processing templates.

Listing 2-14 shows the changes to the `performInitialSetup` function defined in the `default.js` file where I added the call to the `displayListItems` and `setupListEvents` functions after the call to `WinJS.UI.processAll` (and where I removed the code for the previous example from the `performInitialSetup` function).

Listing 2-14. *Ensuring That Elements Are Processed Before Using a Template*

```
...
function performInitialSetup(e) {
  WinJS.UI.processAll().then(function () {
    UI.List.displayListItems();
    UI.List.setupListEvents();
  });
}
...
```

The `processAll` method does its work in the background, allowing the JavaScript statements that follow a call to `processAll` to be executed at the same time. Using background tasks is a good idea, but since my `displayListItems` function relies on the `winControl` property that is created by `processAll`, I need to make sure that the background task has been completed before I use my template.

Understanding Promises

Metro apps rely on the JavaScript *Promise* pattern to represent background tasks. The result from the `processAll` method is a `WinJS.Promise` object, which is the Metro implementation of the JavaScript Promise pattern.

To use the `Promise` object, I call the `then` method on the object, passing in a function that will be executed when the task has completed. In my example, this function makes the calls to the `UI.List` namespace that depend on the `processAll` method having completed its work.

The `then` method takes optional second and third arguments that define functions that will be executed if there is an error and that will receive process information, but for this book I just assume that all background tasks complete properly. I recommend you take the time to handle any errors properly in your own projects.

 Tip   This is the most basic and common use of a JavaScript promise. Take a look at the API definition for the `WinJS.Promise` object to learn about the other capabilities available. Be careful, though; JavaScript promises are a simplified representation of some complex parallel programming concepts, and you can get into a lot of trouble using them if you are not careful. Part of the problem is that JavaScript supports background tasks but doesn't provide the mechanisms required to safely coordinate access to data. This is like providing matches and gas but hiding the fire extinguisher. You *can* use JavaScript promises to create rich parallel-enabled applications, but it requires care and skill.

The final step in applying my template is to add my ui.js file to default.html, as shown in Listing 2-15.

Listing 2-15. *Adding the ui.js File to default.html*

```
...
<link href="/css/list.css" rel="stylesheet">
<link href="/css/default.css" rel="stylesheet">
<script src="/js/viewmodel.js"></script>
<script src="/js/ui.js"></script>
<script src="/js/default.js"></script>
...
```

▨ **Note** As you can see, I have also defined a new stylesheet called list.css. The file contains some simple CSS styles to format the list items and is included as part of the source code download that accompanies this book and that is available without charge from Apress.com.

The WinJS.UI.processAll method sets the CSS display property to none so that the template isn't visible to the user. You can see the result of using the template to populate the table in Figure 2-4.

Figure 2-4. *Generating table rows using a template and a List object*

▨ **Note** I added some styles to default.css to control the appearance of the table. There is nothing specific to Metro in these styles, and you can find the changes in the source code download that accompanies this book (available from Apress.com).

Summary

In this chapter, I showed you how to create a view model in a Metro application, how to make it available globally, and how to make data items observable. The current state of the WinJS API makes this a somewhat awkward process, but the reward is the ability to use declarative bindings and templates to populate your HTML with application data.

Application Controls

For the most part, the user interface controls that you use in a Metro app are the same as the ones you use when creating a regular HTML web app. If you want to gather data from the user, then you can use elements such as `select`, `input`, and `textarea`. If you want to allow the user to commence an action, then you can use `button` elements, and so on. The appearance of these elements in your app is controlled by a combination of the CSS in your project and the capabilities of Internet Explorer 10.

In addition to these basic controls, the WinJS API defines some that are specific to Metro. In this chapter, I show you how to use the most important of these controls, focusing on those that are essential to implementing the Metro app experience, both for the user and for the developer.

I begin by showing you the AppBar and Flyout controls. The AppBar is a core feature of all Metro apps and is the mechanism by which users perform interactions that are not directly possible using the data and controls in the main application layout. Flyouts are a way of providing consistent pop-ups to users and are closely associated with AppBars.

Not all WinJS controls are for the benefit of the user. In this chapter, I show you how to use the HTMLControl to import fragments of HTML into your application. The HTMLControl is useful only for static HTML content, so I also show you how to use the *Pages* feature to load HTML and its associated JavaScript and CSS. These techniques allow for the effective partitioning of application content and functionality, which makes for an easier development experience and simpler testing and maintenance. For completeness, I finish this chapter showing you how to import external content into your Metro app, which can be useful if you have invested in an existing content infrastructure and want to incorporate it into your application. Table 3-1 provides the summary for this chapter.

Adding an AppBar

The *AppBar* appears at the bottom of the screen when the user makes an upward swiping gesture or right-clicks with the mouse. The emphasis in the Metro UI seems to be to have as few controls as is possible on the main layout and rely on the AppBar as the mechanism for any interaction that is not about the immediately available functionality.

I could define the HTML for AppBars directly in `default.html`, but as I mentioned at the start of this chapter, WinJS supports dynamically loading and inserting fragments of HTML.

Table 3-1. *Chapter Summary*

Problem	Solution	Listing
Denote an AppBar.	Define a div element with a data-win-control attribute of WinJS.UI.AppBar.	1, 3, 4
Import a fragment of static content.	Use the HTMLControl feature.	2
Denote a flyout.	Define a div element with a data-win-control attribute of WinJS.UI.Flyout.	5
Associate a flyout with an AppBar button.	Configure the button element so that the type property is flyout and the flyout property is set to the id of the flyout div element.	6
Manage a flyout.	Use the DOM API to manage the controls in the flyout and the members of the flyout div element's winControl property to manage the flyout functionality.	7, 8
Load content into a Metro app.	Create fragments of HTML and use the WinJS.UI.Pages.define method to register a callback function that will be executed when the content is loaded. Use the WinJS.UI.Pages.render method to load the content.	9 through 12
Load HTML, JavaScript, and CSS into a Metro app together.	Create an HTML document and use script and link elements to reference the JavaScript and CSS files. Use the WinJS.UI.Pages.define and WinJS.UI.Pages.render methods to register a callback function and load the document.	13 through 15
Display content that is external to a Metro app.	Use an iframe and ensure that the Internet (Client) permission is declared in the app's manifest.	16 through 18

To demonstrate this feature, I have created an html folder in the Solution Explorer and created an appbar.html file using the HTML Page item in the Add New Item dialog. The contents of appbar.html, which contains the definition of my AppBar, are shown in Listing 3-1.

Tip Ensure that you are not running the debugger when you create the html folder. If you are, Visual Studio will create a folder called NewFolder but won't let you change the name until the debugger has stopped.

Listing 3-1. *Defining an AppBar in the appbar.html File*

```
<div id="appBar" data-win-control="WinJS.UI.AppBar">
  <button data-win-control="WinJS.UI.AppBarCommand"
    data-win-options="{section: 'global', label: 'New Item', icon: 'add'}">
  </button>
  <button data-win-control="WinJS.UI.AppBarCommand"
    data-win-options="{section: 'global', label: 'Stores',
      icon: 'shop'}">
  </button>
  <button data-win-control="WinJS.UI.AppBarCommand"
    data-win-options="{section: 'global', label: 'Zip Code', icon: 'home'}">
  </button>
  <button data-win-control="WinJS.UI.AppBarCommand"
    data-win-options="{id: 'done', disabled: true,
      section: 'selection', label: 'Done', icon: 'accept'}">
  </button>
</div>
```

The AppBar is denoted by a div element that has the data-win-control set to WinJS. AppBar. An AppBar contains one or more button elements whose data-win-control attribute is set to WinJS.UI.AppBarCommand. Each button requires configuration information, and this is provided through the data-win-options attribute, following the format of a simple JavaScript object. I'll explain the meaning of the configuration properties shortly.

Tip   You can also specify AppBar buttons using a series of nested HTML elements, which obviates the need for the JavaScript-like configuration object. I don't like having to embed fragments of code into my markup, but it is something that pervades WinJS, so I tend to stick with the approach shown in the listing. It is ugly, but it is consistent with the way other controls work.

Listing 3-2 shows how I import the HTML fragment defined in appbar.html into the default.html document.

Listing 3-2. *Importing an HTML Fragment into default.html*

```
<!DOCTYPE html>
<html>
<head>
  <meta charset="utf-8">
  <title>MetroGrocer</title>
  <!-- WinJS references -->
  <link href="//Microsoft.WinJS.0.6/css/ui-dark.css" rel="stylesheet">
  <script src="//Microsoft.WinJS.0.6/js/base.js"></script>
  <script src="//Microsoft.WinJS.0.6/js/ui.js"></script>
  <!-- MetroGrocer references -->
  <link href="/css/list.css" rel="stylesheet">
  <link href="/css/default.css" rel="stylesheet">
```

```
  <script src="/js/viewmodel.js"></script>
  <script src="/js/ui.js"></script>
  <script src="/js/default.js"></script>
</head>
<body>
  <div id="contentGrid">
    <div id="leftContainer" class="gridLeft">
      <h1 class="win-type-xx-large">Grocery List</h1>

      <table id="listTable" class="type-table-header">
        <thead>
          <tr>
            <th>Quantity</th>
            <th class="itemName">Item</th>
            <th class="store">Store</th>
          </tr>
        </thead>
        <tbody id="itemBody"></tbody>
      </table>
    </div>
    <div id="topRightContainer" class="gridRight">
      <h1 class="win-type-xx-large">Top Right Container</h1>
    </div>
    <div id="bottomRightContainer" class="gridRight">
      <h1 class="win-type-xx-large">Bottom Right Container</h1>
    </div>
  </div>

  <!-- import HTML fragments -->
  <div data-win-control="WinJS.UI.HtmlControl"
    data-win-options="{uri: '/html/appbar.html'}"></div>
  <!-- end of HTML fragments -->

  <!-- template for grocery list items -->
  <table>
    <tbody id="itemTemplate" data-win-control="WinJS.Binding.Template">
      <tr class="groceryItem">
        <td data-win-bind="innerText: quantity"></td>
        <td data-win-bind="innerText: item"></td>
        <td data-win-bind="innerText: store"></td>
      </tr>
    </tbody>
  </table>
  <!-- end of template for grocery list items -->
</body>
</html>
```

When you call the WinJS.UI.processAll method, WinJS finds all div elements whose data-win-control attribute is set to WinJS.UI.HtmlControl and sets their content to the HTML fragment specified in the data-win-options attribute. You can't specify the fragment file directly; instead, you have to use the JavaScript-like format I have shown in the listing, specifying the file name as the value for the `uri` property.

Tip The `HTMLControl` is only for loading fragments of content that don't need to execute script or define any CSS. This works in my example because the JavaScript that sets up the AppBar from the HTML fragment is part of `default.js`, which is already associated with the main HTML document. And, as I describe in a moment, I have to take precautions to make sure that the HTML fragment is loaded before performing the AppBar setup. Later in this chapter, I show you WinJS *pages*, which support their own CSS and JavaScript.

The contents of the loaded file are processed automatically, and WinJS finds and configures my AppBar. You don't have to worry about making the AppBar appear and disappear. This is configured by WinJS, and the AppBar will appear when the user right-clicks or swipes up from the bottom of the screen. You can see how the AppBar appears in Figure 3-1.

Figure 3-1. *Adding an AppBar to the example application*

I have magnified a couple of the buttons in the figure to make them easier to see the effect of the configuration properties applied to each AppBar button. The `id` and `disabled` properties set the corresponding attributes on the `button` element, and the `label` property sets the text displayed underneath the button.

There are two regions on an AppBar, and the `section` property specifies which one a button appears in. If the `section` property is set to `global`, then the `button` will be toward the right side of the AppBar. This area is for actions that affect the entire application. A button whose section is `selection` performs actions that apply to the currently selected item and are displayed on the left of the AppBar.

The `icon` property sets the `button` image. You can specify a custom PNG file for this property or use one of the symbol characters defined in the Segoe UI Symbol font. You can refer to these icons either by specifying one of the values from the `WinJS.UI.AppBarIcon` enumeration or directly by its character code (which you can get using the Windows 8 Character Map tool). As an example, I specified the add icon for one of the buttons, which corresponds to the `WinJS.UI.AppBarIcon.add` value or the character code `\uE109`.

Tip There are a lot of icons to choose from, far more than the API documentation suggests. Open the `js/ui.js` file and search for `icon` to see the list defined by the enumeration. The enumeration just contains common icons; there are even more defined by the font itself.

Implementing App Bar Buttons

In this section, I will add the code to implement the selection-specific Done button I added to the AppBar. To do this, I have defined a `UI.AppBar` namespace in the `ui.js` file and created the `setupButtons` function, which you can see in Listing 3-3.

Listing 3-3. *Setting Up Support for the AppBar Buttons*

```
/// <reference path="//Microsoft.WinJS.0.6/js/base.js" />
/// <reference path="//Microsoft.WinJS.0.6/js/ui.js" />

(function () {
  "use strict";

  WinJS.Namespace.define("UI.AppBar", {
    setupButtons: function () {
      var doneButton = document.getElementById("done");
      ViewModel.State.bind("selectedItemIndex", function (newValue, oldValue) {
        doneButton.disabled = (newValue == -1);
      });

      doneButton.addEventListener("click", function (e) {
        var selectedIndex = ViewModel.State.selectedItemIndex;
        ViewModel.UserData.getItems().splice(selectedIndex, 1);
        ViewModel.State.selectedItemIndex = -1;
      });
    }
  });

  WinJS.Namespace.define("UI.List", {
    // ...code removed for brevity...
  });
})();
```

Since AppBar buttons are created from HTML button elements, I can use the standard disabled property to control the button state and handle the click event to respond to user interaction.

I want to control the state of the button in response to changes to the `ViewModel.State.selectedItemIndex` property in the view model. To monitor an object with observable properties, you use the bind method to register a function that will be executed when the value the property changes. In this listing, I have created a binding for the `selectedItemIndex` property so that I can change the status of the button when the user makes a selection. This is a nice demonstration of how you can use WinJS data bindings to tie view model data, event handler functions, and HTML elements together.

The last step is to call the `setupButtons` function from within `performInitialSetup` in the `default.js` file, as shown in Listing 3-4. Notice that, once again, I make the call to my function within the then callback provided by the `Promise` object so that I can be sure that my HTML fragment has been loaded and processed before I start performing operations on the elements it contains.

Listing 3-4. *Calling the setupButtons Function*

```
...
function performInitialSetup(e) {
  WinJS.UI.processAll().then(function () {
    UI.List.displayListItems();
    UI.List.setupListEvents();
    UI.AppBar.setupButtons();
  });
}
...
```

And, with these additions, I have a basic AppBar in place. If you select an item in the grocery list, the Done button will be enabled, allowing you to reveal the AppBar and mark the item as completed, removing it from the list. I am not going to implement functionality for all of the AppBar buttons, but in the following section I'll wire up the Add button so that I can demonstrate how to create and use a Flyout.

Adding Flyouts

Flyouts are pop-up windows that you can use to provide information to, or gather data from, the user. Flyouts are often used in conjunction with AppBar buttons, and in this section I show you how to use a flyout to complete the Add Item AppBar button. To begin, I have created a new file in the `html` folder called `addItemFlyout.html`, the contents of which are shown in Listing 3-5.

Listing 3-5. *Defining a Flyout*

```
<div class="flyout" id="addItemFlyout" data-win-control="WinJS.UI.Flyout">
  <div>
    <label for="item">Item:</label>
    <input id="item" placeholder="e.g. Apples">
  </div>
  <div>
    <label for="quantity">Quantity:</label>
    <input id="quantity" placeholder="e.g. 4"/>
  </div>
  <div>
    <label for="stores">Store:</label>
    <select id="stores"></select>
  </div>
  <div class="rightAlign">
    <button id="addItemButton">Add</button>
  </div>
</div>
```

Flyouts are denoted by a div element whose data-win-control attribute is set to WinJS. UI.Flyout. This is the only limitation to creating a flyout, and I am free to add any content inside the div element that I need to support my interaction with the user. In this example, I have used some standard HTML form controls to gather details of the new item from the user.

Tip   If you are used to developing web apps, you will be accustomed to building data-gathering interactions around the HTML form element. In a Metro app, the form element is that important because the majority of interactions are handled entirely within the client. That said, you can still use the form element with Ajax requests if you want to submit data to a server.

Having defined the flyout, I can now associate it with my AppBar, which I do by adding configuration properties to the button element in the appbar.html file, as shown in Listing 3-6.

Listing 3-6. *Associating a Flyout with an AppBar Button*

```
...
<button data-win-control="WinJS.UI.AppBarCommand"
  data-win-options="{section: 'global', label: 'New Item', icon: 'add',
    type:'flyout', flyout: 'addItemFlyout'}">
</button>
...
```

To specify the flyout associated with the button, I set the type property to flyout and the flyout property to the id of the flyout element. When the user clicks the button, my flyout is automatically displayed, as shown in Figure 3-2.

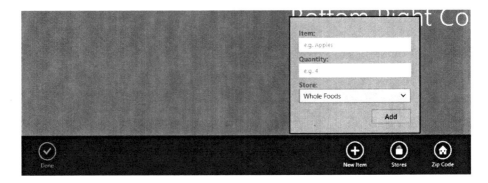

Figure 3-2. *Associating a flyout with an AppBar button*

Tip   A type value of toggle creates an AppBar button that the user can switch on or off. A value of button is equivalent to not setting a type property at all, and AppBar buttons work just like regular HTML buttons (as demonstrated earlier in this chapter).

To bring my flyout HTML fragment into the application, I have to update `default.html` and make use of `HTMLControl` again:

```
...
<!-- import HTML fragments -->
<div data-win-control="WinJS.UI.HtmlControl"
  data-win-options="{uri: '/html/appbar.html'}"></div>
<div data-win-control="WinJS.UI.HtmlControl"
  data-win-options="{uri: '/html/addItemFlyout.html'}"></div>
<!-- end of HTML fragments -->
...
```

Tip To style the flyout, I added a new CSS file to the project called `flyouts.css` and added a `link` element to `default.html` to import the styles it contains into the Metro app. The styles are very simple, and you can see them by downloading the source code that accompanies this book from Apress.com.

Managing the Controls in a Flyout

I have shown the fully implemented flyout in Figure 3-2, but getting to this point requires some additional code. I need to populate the `select` element with details of the stores in the view model and handle the `click` event for the Add button so that the new item is added to the list. Listing 3-7 shows the changes to the UI namespace in the `ui.js` file to handle both of these areas.

Listing 3-7. *Adding Support for the Flyout Controls to the UI Namespace*

```
/// <reference path="//Microsoft.WinJS.0.6/js/base.js" />
/// <reference path="//Microsoft.WinJS.0.6/js/ui.js" />
(function () {
  "use strict";

  WinJS.Namespace.define("UI.Flyouts", {
    setupAddItemFlyout: function () {

      var selectElement = WinJS.Utilities.query('select#stores')[0];
      WinJS.Utilities.empty(selectElement);
      var list = ViewModel.UserData.getStores();
      list.forEach(function (item) {
        var newOption = document.createElement("option");
        newOption.text = item;
        selectElement.add(newOption);
      });

      document.getElementById("addItemButton").addEventListener("click",
        function () {
          var item =
            WinJS.Utilities.query("#addItemFlyout #item")[0].value;
          var quantity =
            WinJS.Utilities.query("#addItemFlyout #quantity")[0].value;
```

```
            var store=WinJS.Utilities.query("#addItemFlyout #stores")[0].value;
            ViewModel.UserData.addItem(item, quantity, store);
            document.getElementById("addItemFlyout").winControl.hide();
            document.getElementById("appBar").winControl.hide();
        });
    }
});
// ... other namespace definitions omitted for brevity
})();
```

I have created a UI.Flyouts object that defines the setupAddItemFlyout function. This function populates the select control from the view model, and when the Add button is clicked, it reads the values from the input and select elements and uses them to create a item in the grocery list.

When I am done with the flyout, I locate the div element and use the winControl property to get the WinJS members that are specific to flyouts. The hide method dismisses the flyout and returns the user to the main layout. I perform the same task on the AppBar element, which would otherwise be left visible when the flyout is closed. See the WinJS API documentation for details of the other methods available through the winControl property of AppBar and flyout elements.

Of course, defining this code isn't enough; I have to call the function from the default.js file, as shown in Listing 3-8.

Listing 3-8. *Calling the Code to Set Up the Flyout Controls*

```
...
function performInitialSetup(e) {
  WinJS.UI.processAll().then(function () {
    UI.List.displayListItems();
    UI.List.setupListEvents();
    UI.AppBar.setupButtons();
    UI.Flyouts.setupAddItemFlyout();
  });
}
...
```

Using Pages

Earlier in the chapter, I used HTMLControl to import fragments into my main HTML document. The main limitation in using HTMLControl is that you can't arrange to be notified when your content is loaded. This is fine for content when you are using fragments just to reuse regions of markup, but the HTMLControl isn't much help if you want to load content fragments dynamically in response to user input.

HTMLControl is a simple declarative wrapper around a more complex WinJS feature called *pages*. Pages must be set up and managed in JavaScript, but they provide a richer set of functions and, crucially, support callbacks that can be used to integrate content at any point in the application's life cycle.

> ▨ **Caution** The pages feature is pretty raw, and it looks like they were a late addition to the Windows 8 Consumer Preview, replacing a similar feature that was incredibly difficult to use. This is an area that I suspect will change again before the final Windows 8 release.

To demonstrate the pages feature, I am going to implement the top-right region of the layout, allowing the user to edit the contents of the currently selected item and display a useful message when no selection has been made.

I need do to three things to use a page. The first is to define the HTML, the second is to write the JavaScript that will be executed when the HTML is loaded, and the third thing is to load and display the HTML as part of the application.

Defining the HTML

For the first step, I have created a file called noSelection.html in the html folder of the project. The contents of this file are shown in Listing 3-9. This is the markup that will be displayed to the user when no grocery list item has been selected.

Listing 3-9. *The noSelection.html File*

```html
<div id="noselectionContainer" class="win-type-x-large">
  <p>There are <span id="numberCount"></span>items on your list</p>
  <p>Select to edit</p>
</div>
```

This is the complete content of the HTML file; it contains just the elements I want to insert into the document, which is the same approach when I used the HTMLControl feature previously. I'll show you how to use complete HTML documents shortly, but I wanted to emphasize that the pages feature will quite happily operate on fragments of markup, which is how I tend to break up my applications.

Creating the JavaScript Callback

The second step is to define the code that will be executed when the HTML is loaded. Remember, this is the main benefit of using the pages feature; I can rely on the code I specify being executed every time I display the fragment, allowing me to configure the elements to match the present state of the app. Listing 3-10 shows the contents of the pages.js file, which I created in the js folder.

Listing 3-10. *Defining the Code to Be Executed When a Page Fragment Is Loaded*

```javascript
/// <reference path="//Microsoft.WinJS.0.6/js/base.js" />
/// <reference path="//Microsoft.WinJS.0.6/js/ui.js" />

(function () {
  "use strict";

  WinJS.UI.Pages.define("/html/noselection.html", {
```

```
    ready: function (targetElement) {
      document.getElementById("numberCount").innerText
        = ViewModel.UserData.getItems().length;
    }
  });
})();
```

The callback function is set up through the WinJS.UI.Pages.define method. The arguments are the URL of the HTML file that will be loaded and an object whose properties define the functions that will be executed when this happens. In the Consumer Preview, the only property that works reliably is ready, and the function assigned to this property will be executed when the HTML has been loaded and processed by the Metro runtime.

In this example, my ready callback function locates the span element in the noSelection.html markup and sets its content to be the number of items on the grocery list. I have added a script element to the default.html file to load pages.js:

```
...
<!-- MetroGrocer references -->
<link href="/css/list.css" rel="stylesheet">
<link href="/css/flyouts.css" rel="stylesheet">
<link href="/css/default.css" rel="stylesheet">
<script src="/js/viewmodel.js"></script>
<script src="/js/ui.js"></script>
<script src="/js/pages.js"></script>
<script src="/js/default.js"></script>
...
```

Loading and Displaying the HTML

The define method doesn't load the HTML; it just sets up the callbacks. To display the content, I need to pick a place to insert it in the default.html file. You can see the addition in Listing 3-11. No special attributes are required for the placeholder; a regular div element will do, ideally with an id attribute so you can easily locate it later.

Listing 3-11. Adding a Page Placeholder Element in default.html

```
...
<div id="topRightContainer" class="gridRight">
  <h1 class="win-type-xx-large">Item Detail</h1>
  <div id="itemDetailTarget"></div>
</div>
...
```

The final step is to display the page within the target element. You can see the additions to the default.js file in Listing 3-12.

Listing 3-12. Loading a WinJS Page

```
...
function performInitialSetup(e) {
  WinJS.UI.processAll().then(function () {
```

```
    UI.List.displayListItems();
    UI.List.setupListEvents();
    UI.AppBar.setupButtons();
    UI.Flyouts.setupAddItemFlyout();

    var targetElement = document.getElementById("itemDetailTarget");
    WinJS.Utilities.empty(targetElement)
    WinJS.UI.Pages.render("/html/noSelection.html", targetElement);
  });
}
...
```

The first two lines locate the placeholder element and remove any child elements that already exist there. The final statement is the important one: I display the page by calling the WinJS.UI.Pages.render method. The arguments to this method are the URL of the HTML document and the placeholder element where the content will be inserted.

When I call the render method, WinJS not only inserts the HTML from the specified file into the document but ensures that my callback function, the one I defined in pages.js, is executed. This allows me to process the elements, in this case, to insert details about how many items are on the grocery list, as shown in Figure 3-3.

Figure 3-3. *Using a page to associate a callback function with a fragment of HTML*

Loading a Complete HTML Document

A variation on the page example is to work with complete HTML documents, rather than fragments. The basic approach is the same, but I can include script and link elements to load JavaScript and CSS files that are specific to the document. This means I can keep my callback definition code and CSS styles separate from the rest of the application. To begin, I create a new folder called pages and another one called itemDetail inside it. I then add a new HTML file called itemDetail.html, which is shown in Listing 3-13.

Listing 3-13. *The itemDetail.html File*

```
<!DOCTYPE html>
<html>
<head>
  <title></title>
  <script src="itemDetail.js"></script>
  <link href="itemDetail.css" rel="stylesheet">
</head>
```

```
<body>
  <div id="itemEditor">
    <div>
      <label for="item">Item:</label><input id="item">
    </div>
    <div>
      <label for="quantity">Quantity:</label><input id="quantity">
    </div>
    <div>
      <label for="stores">Store:</label>
      <select id="stores" size="3"></select>
    </div>
  </div>
</body>
</html>
```

The markup in this file provides a `select` and two `input` elements to allow the user to edit the details of a grocery list item. The difference from the previous example is that this is a complete HTML document that contains a `script` element that imports the `itemDetail.js` file and a `link` element that imports the `itemDetail.css` file, both of which I have created in the same `pages/itemDetail` folder, alongside `itemDetail.html`.

Tip   The `itemDetail.css` file just contains some basic CSS styles; you can see these in the source code download if you are interested, but there is nothing new or Metro-specific to see.

The `itemDetail.js` file contains the callback for when the page is loaded, as shown in Listing 3-14.

Listing 3-14. *Defining the Page Callback for the itemDetail.html Page*

```
/// <reference path="//Microsoft.WinJS.0.6/js/base.js" />
/// <reference path="//Microsoft.WinJS.0.6/js/ui.js" />

(function () {
  "use strict";

  WinJS.UI.Pages.define("/pages/itemDetail/itemDetail.html", {
    ready: function (targetElement) {

      var selectedIndex = ViewModel.State.selectedItemIndex;
      var selectedItem = ViewModel.UserData.getItems().getAt(selectedIndex);

      document.getElementById("item").value = selectedItem.item;
      document.getElementById("quantity").value = selectedItem.quantity;

      var selectElement = WinJS.Utilities.query('select#stores')[0];
      WinJS.Utilities.empty(selectElement);
      var list = ViewModel.UserData.getStores();
      list.forEach(function (item) {
        var newOption = document.createElement("option");
```

```
          newOption.text = item;
          if (selectedItem.store == item) {
            newOption.selected = true;
          }
          selectElement.add(newOption);
        });

        WinJS.Utilities.query('#itemEditor input, #itemEditor select')
          .listen("change", function () {

          ViewModel.UserData.getItems().setAt(selectedIndex, {
            item: document.getElementById("item").value,
            quantity: document.getElementById("quantity").value,
            store: document.getElementById("stores").value
          });
        });
      }
    })
  })();
```

When I call the define method, I have to specify the *complete* path to the HTML document that I want to be notified about. This means pages/itemDetail/itemDetail.html rather than just itemDetail.html. This is different from the links to the CSS and JavaScript files defined inside itemDetail.html, which are relative (i.e., just itemDetail.js).

Since the Metro runtime for JavaScript apps is essentially a regular browser, the JavaScript code is executed as soon as the script element is processed. This means that the callback function is registered before the document has been completely loaded and will then be called once the document has been completely processed. This provides the foundation for a nice way to keep pages self-contained, and you don't need to have the callbacks defined alongside the main app code.

The callback function in this example is pretty simple and just uses the values from the input and select elements to modify the list of grocery items using the WinJS.Binding.List. setAt method. The setAt method completely replaces the item in the list and triggers an item-changed event, which I showed you in Chapter 2. This event causes the table element display-ing the list items to be updated with the changes the user has made.

Tip Since this page is a complete HTML document, you can reference multiple JavaScript and CSS files; in fact, if you create a new Page item from the Add ➤ New Item menu, Visual Studio will create an HTML file, a JavaScript file, and a CSS file and link them together.

Switching Between Pages

Now that I have two pages, I can switch between them in the main layout. I want to display the noSelection.html page when no item has been selected and the itemDetail.html page when a selection has been made. The simplest way to arrange this is to bind to the ViewModel.State. selectedItemIndex property. Listing 3-15 shows the changes in the default.js file.

Listing 3-15. *Switching Between Two Pages in Response to a View Model Update*

```
...
function performInitialSetup(e) {
  WinJS.UI.processAll().then(function () {
    UI.List.displayListItems();
    UI.List.setupListEvents();
    UI.AppBar.setupButtons();
    UI.Flyouts.setupAddItemFlyout();

    ViewModel.State.bind("selectedItemIndex", function (newValue) {
      var targetElement = document.getElementById("itemDetailTarget");
      WinJS.Utilities.empty(targetElement)
      var url = newValue == -1 ? "/html/noSelection.html" :
        "/pages/itemDetail/itemDetail.html"
      WinJS.UI.Pages.render(url, targetElement);
    });
  });
}
...
```

I respond to changes in the selectedItemIndex property by altering the value of the URL argument I pass to the WinJS.UI.Pages.render method. Each time a page is displayed, the relevant callback function is executed, and my content is updated and presented to the user.

Tip Note that when you use the bind method, your callback function will be executed with the current value of the property you are monitoring. This allows me to ensure that the correct page is displayed, even when the user has yet to make a selection.

The result of these additions is that clicking an item in the list allows the user to edit its details, while marking the item done or adding a new item clears the selection and hides the detail page. You can see the effect in Figure 3-4.

The code in the callback for a page is executed *every time* that page is displayed. You need to ensure that your code doesn't make assumptions about the state of the elements in your page, other than they have been loaded and added to the main layout. Since a page is loaded within the context of the main layout, you can safely use the functions defined by JavaScript code used by the main HTML document. In my example, this includes the view model. Similarly, your elements will be subject to the CSS styles that the main document defines.

Figure 3-4. *Allowing the user to edit the details of a grocery list item*

> **Tip** Notice that I have used the `size` attribute on the `select` element so that several choices are shown at once. This is the Metro convention for `select` elements that are part of the main application layout. However, for flyouts, such as the one I created earlier in this chapter, the convention is a single-line `select` that opens a drop-down list of options.

Displaying External Content

The WinJS page feature works only on content that is part of the application. You will generate an error if you request an external URL using the `WinJS.UI.Pages.render` method. Instead, you must use an `iframe` element if you want to display an external HTML document, but you can combine this element with the WinJS page feature if you want to get the benefit of breaking your application down into small and manageable pieces. To demonstrate this, I have created a new file in the `html` directory called `storeDetail.html`. Listing 3-16 shows the contents of this file.

Listing 3-16. *The storeDetail.html File*

```
<!DOCTYPE html>
<html>
  <head>
    <title></title>
  </head>
  <body>
    <div id="noStoreSelectionContainer" class="win-type-x-large">
      <p>Select an item on the list</p>
    </div>

    <div id="storeSelectionContainer">
      <iframe id="storeFrame" seamless sandbox=""></iframe>
    </div>
  </body>
</html>
```

This is a simple document that acts as a wrapper around the `iframe` element and a placeholder element to display when no list item has been selected. The most important element is, of course, the `iframe`. The `seamless` attribute specifies that no border should be drawn around the `iframe`, and setting the `sandbox` attribute to the empty string prevents the embedded content from running any scripts, navigating to new pages, and submitting forms. I am going to use the `iframe` to display the home page of the grocery store associated with the selected item. These pages contain all sorts of tracking scripts and some very exception-prone code, all of which I want to spare my user from having to deal with.

Adding the Callback

I am going to use the same approach for defining a callback as I did when loading a fragment. I have added the callback function to the `pages.js` file, and you can see the additions in Listing 3-17.

Listing 3-17. *Defining a Callback for the Page*

```
/// <reference path="//Microsoft.WinJS.0.6/js/base.js" />
/// <reference path="//Microsoft.WinJS.0.6/js/ui.js" />

(function () {
  "use strict";

  WinJS.UI.Pages.define("/html/noselection.html", {
    ready: function (targetElement) {
      document.getElementById("numberCount").innerText
        = ViewModel.UserData.getItems().length;
    }
  });

  WinJS.UI.Pages.define("/html/storeDetail.html", {
    ready: function (targetElement) {
      ViewModel.State.bind("selectedItemIndex", function (newValue) {

        document.getElementById('noStoreSelectionContainer').style.display
          = (newValue != -1 ? "none" : "");
        document.getElementById('storeSelectionContainer').style.display
          = (newValue == -1 ? "none" : "");

        if (newValue != -1) {
          var store = ViewModel.UserData.getItems().getAt(newValue).store;
          var url = "http://" + store.replace(" ", "") + ".com";
          document.getElementById("storeFrame").src = url;
        }
      });
    }
  });
})
})();
```

In the ready callback for this page, I bind to the selectedItemIndex property. When the user selects an item, I use the iframe to display the home page of the relevant store. Changing the value of the style.display property lets me switch between the placeholder element and the detail for the current store.

Tip   My technique to creating a URL from a store name is pretty basic. I just remove any spaces and add .com to the end of the name. This won't suffice for a real project, but it will do just fine for my simple example.

Showing the Page

You must avoid using ready callbacks to set up bindings for pages that are not always displayed, because the JavaScript code will be executed each time the page is loaded. Over time, you end up with a series of bindings, all of which perform the same task. WinJS doesn't provide a mechanism for cleaning up when the content of a page is removed from the layout, so the best approach is to move bindings into the main JavaScript files for the application.

This isn't a problem for the storeDetails.html page because it is loaded only once and never removed from the document. In this case, I am using the WinJS page feature only so that I can decompose my Metro app into self-contained pieces to make development and mainte-nance easier. As you can see in Listing 3-18, I display the storeDetails.html page just once, meaning that I can expect the code in my callback to be executed just once as well.

Listing 3-18. *Displaying the Page*

```
...
function performInitialSetup(e) {
  WinJS.UI.processAll().then(function () {
    UI.List.displayListItems();
    UI.List.setupListEvents();
    UI.AppBar.setupButtons();
    UI.Flyouts.setupAddItemFlyout();

    ViewModel.State.bind("selectedItemIndex", function (newValue) {
      var targetElement = document.getElementById("itemDetailTarget");
      WinJS.Utilities.empty(targetElement)
      var url = newValue == -1 ? "/html/noSelection.html"
        : "/pages/itemDetail/itemDetail.html"
      WinJS.UI.Pages.render(url, targetElement);
    });

    WinJS.UI.Pages.render("/html/storeDetail.html",
      document.getElementById("storeDetailTarget"));
  });
}
...
```

The final step is to update the layout element in default.html, as follows:

```
...
<div id="bottomRightContainer" class="gridRight">
  <h1 class="win-type-xx-large">Store Detail</h1>
  <div id="storeDetailTarget"></div>
</div>
...
```

The result is that selecting an item on the main list will display the home page of the rel-evant store, as shown in Figure 3-5.

Checking Manifest Permissions

Metro applications are subject to a security sandbox. To obtain access to external content, your application must be granted one or more permissions in its manifest file. To ensure you have the access you need, open the package.appmanifest file from the Solution Explorer and go to the Capabilities tab.

You will see a list of capabilities that you can request. These are presented to the user when they view your app in the Metro Store so that they can make an informed choice about what access they grant to your application. (Well, that's the theory; in practice, users don't generally pay attention to these declarations until an app does something that surprises them.)

Figure 3-5. *Displaying external content*

For the Visual Studio beta, the Internet (Client) capability is checked by default, but you may also require the Private Networks (Client & Server) capability, depending on where your content is coming from. Check the capabilities you require and save the manifest. We'll return to the manifest in Chapter 4 to configure some of the other settings.

■ **Caution**   This is an area that I expect to change before the final Windows 8 release. The idea of private and public networks is expressed in the Metro manifest capabilities, but not in the operating system when the user sets up network connections. For the Consumer Preview at least, all network connections are treated the same way, so the capabilities for a Metro app and the network model for the operating system will have to converge at some point.

Summary

In this chapter, I introduced three important structural features for a Metro app: AppBars, flyouts, and the navigation model. These facilities start to bridge the gap between a generic web app and the tools for decomposing your application into manageable chunks.

You don't have to use AppBars and flyouts, but your application won't fit into the Metro model if you don't. Part of the attraction of Metro is to be able to use your HTML5 and JavaScript skills to create Windows applications. Creating an app that doesn't follow the Metro conventions is to miss the opportunity that Windows 8 presents to the web programmer.

Equally, you could elect to build your Metro app using a single HTML document. But, once again, this would be a missed opportunity. The constraints that drive web apps toward content consolidation don't exist for Metro apps, which means that the ease of development, testing, and maintenance that come from decomposing your content and code are worth exploring. The HTMLControl and pages features are key enablers to this development style.

Layouts and Tiles

In this chapter, I describe two of the features that allow a Metro app to fit into the wider user experience presented by Windows 8. The first of these features is the way that Metro apps can be *snapped* and *filled* so that two apps can be viewed side by side. I show you how to adapt when your app is placed into one of these layouts and how to change the layout when your interactions don't fit inside the layout constraints.

The second feature is the Metro *tile* model. Tiles are at the heart of the Windows 8 replacement for the Start menu. At their simplest, they are static buttons that can be used to launch your app, but with a little work they can present the user with an invaluable snapshot of the state of your application, allowing the user to get an overview without having to run the application itself. In this chapter, I show you how to create *live tiles* by applying updates and by using a related feature, *badges*. Table 4-1 provides the summary for this chapter.

Table 4-1. *Chapter Summary*

Problem	Solution	Listing
Adapt an app's layout when it has been placed into a snapped or filled layout.	Use CSS media queries with Metro-specific properties.	1
Detect changes in an app's layout in code or attempt to change the layout.	Use the `Windows.UI.ViewManagement` namespace.	2
Define an update for a tile.	Use an XML tile template.	3
Apply an update to a tile.	Use the `Windows.UI.Notifications` namespace.	4 through 6
Update square and wide tiles.	Populate and combine two XML tile templates.	7, 8
Apply a badge to a tile.	Populate and apply an XML badge template.	9, 10

Dealing with Metro Layouts

Metro apps can be *snapped* into a 320-pixel strip of the screen so that the user can see two applications at once. The other app, which occupies all of the display aside from those 320 pixels, is said to be *filled*. Ensuring that your application can adapt to being snapped and filled is essential to providing the full Metro experience to your users. There are two mechanisms for responding to being filled or snapped; you can use CSS or use the `Windows.UI.ViewManagement` API. I'll show you both approaches in the sections that follow.

Note Applications can be snapped in the landscape view only, and Windows 8 Consumer Preview supports snapping only if the horizontal resolution of the display is 1366 pixels or greater. You must ensure that you have selected the correct orientation and resolution in the simulator if you want to experiment with snapping.

Snapping and Filling with CSS

Microsoft has added some custom CSS media query properties that can be used to change the CSS for a Metro app when it is snapped or filled. These are added to the `default.css` file when Visual Studio creates a new Metro application project, as shown in Listing 4-1.

Listing 4-1. The Custom Snapped and Filled Media Query Properties

```
/* MetroGrocer styles removed for brevity */
@media screen and (-ms-view-state: fullscreen-landscape) {
}

@media screen and (-ms-view-state: filled) {
}

@media screen and (-ms-view-state: snapped) {
  #contentGrid div.gridRight, #listTable td:last-child, #listTable th {
    display: none;
  }

  #listTable td { white-space: nowrap;}

  #listTable td:first-child { border-right: thin solid white;}

  #contentGrid div.gridLeft { margin-left: 0.5em;}
}

@media screen and (-ms-view-state: fullscreen-portrait) {
}
```

The four media queries defined in `default.css` define the four basic layout states that a Metro app can find itself in: snapped, filled, full-screen in landscape mode, and full-screen in portrait mode. The CSS styles I define within the media queries are applied only when the app is in the corresponding state.

For my example application, the snapped view presents too little space to display the entire layout. As you can see in the listing, I have used the snapped media query to hide some elements and change the appearance and behavior of others. You can see how these styles are applied in the snapped view in Figure 4-1.

Tip The normal CSS precedence rules apply to styles defined within these queries, which means that you would normally want to make the `link` element for the `default.css` file the last one to appear in the `default.html` file.

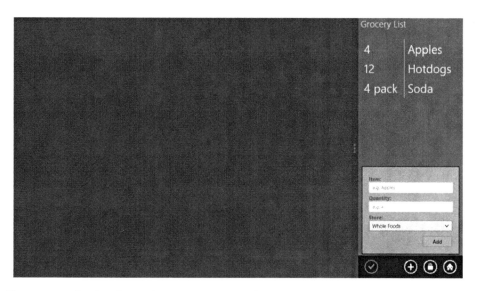

Figure 4-1. *Adapting the app layout using CSS media queries*

I have shown the snapped view next to an empty panel, but usually there would be another application occupying this space. Notice that Windows adapts the Metro structural elements automatically, such as removing the labels from AppBar buttons in the snapped layout.

Snapping and Filling with JavaScript

You can do a surprising amount to adapt to different layouts using just CSS, but there comes a point where you need to be able to adapt in JavaScript as well. The Windows.UI.ViewManagement namespace defines an object called ApplicationView that provides details about the current layout and provides a simple mechanism for trying to change it. To demonstrate this feature, I have modified the displayListItems method defined in my ui.js file, as shown in Listing 4-2.

Listing 4-2. *Adapting to Layouts Using JavaScript*

```
...
displayListItems: function () {

  var templateElement = document.getElementById("itemTemplate");
  var targetElement = document.getElementById("itemBody");

  WinJS.Utilities.empty(targetElement);

  var list = ViewModel.UserData.getItems();

  for (var i = 0; i < list.length; i++) {
    templateElement.winControl.render(list.getAt(i), targetElement);
  }

  ViewModel.State.bind("selectedItemIndex", function (newIndex) {
    var children = WinJS.Utilities.children(targetElement).
```

```
removeClass("selected");
    if (newIndex > -1 && newIndex < children.length) {
      WinJS.Utilities.addClass(children[newIndex], "selected");

      var appview = Windows.UI.ViewManagement.ApplicationView;
      if (appview.value == Windows.UI.ViewManagement.ApplicationViewState.snapped){
        appview.tryUnsnap();
      }
    }
  });

  WinJS.Utilities.children(targetElement).listen("click", function (e) {
    ViewModel.State.selectedItemIndex = this.rowIndex - 1;
  });
},
...
```

I have refactored this function so that rows are selected in response to changes in the ViewModel.State.selectedItemIndex property and not just when the user clicks one of the rows in the table element. This gives me an ideal opportunity to check the layout of the app using the ApplicationView object. The effect I want is that if the user selects an item while the application is snapped, then I change the layout to give myself enough space to show the elements for editing the item details and viewing the web site of the appropriate store.

The ApplicationView.value property returns the current layout, represented by a value from the ApplicationViewState enumeration. The values are snapped, filled, fullScreenPortrait, and fullScreenLandscape.

If my app layout is snapped, then I call the tryUnsnap method. This will unsnap the application. The result seems to be a little inconsistent in the Consumer Preview release; sometimes my application is switched to the filled layout and other times to the full-screen layout.

Tip The ApplicationView object defines an addEventListener method that you can use to register a handler for the viewstatechanged event. Your handler will be executed whenever the layout changes.

Using Tiles and Badges

Tiles are the representation of your application on the Start menu. At their simplest, tiles are just static icons for starting your app. However, with a little effort, you can use your tile to present the user with a useful summary of your app's state and to draw their attention to activities they may want to perform.

In the sections that follow, I demonstrate how to present information through the tile of my example Metro app. There are two possible, and conflicting, goals when you create a live tile; you are trying to either encourage the user to run your app or dissuade them from running it. If you are trying to attract the user, then your tile becomes an ad for the experience, insights, or content you offer. This is appropriate for entertainment apps or those that present external content such as news.

Dissuading the user from running an app may seem like a strange goal, but it can significantly improve the user experience. Consider productivity apps as an example. I dread to think the hours I have lost waiting for calendar or to-do apps to load, just so I can check where my next appointment is or what my most urgent action requires. You can reduce the friction and frustration that your users experience when using your app and create a more pleasing and immediate experience by displaying the information that the user needs in your app tile.

Both goals require careful thought. The overall Metro experience is flat, simple, and sub-dued. If you are using your tile as an ad, then the muted nature of Metro makes it easy to create tiles that stand out. If you go too far, though, you will create something that is discordant and jarring and is more of an eyesore than an attraction.

If your goal is to reduce the number of times the user needs to run your app, then you need to present the right information at the right time. This requires a good understanding of what drives your users to adopt your app and the ability to customize the data that is presented. Adaptability is essential; there is no point showing me the most urgent work action on my task list on a Saturday morning, for example. Every time you present the user with the wrong infor-mation, you force them to run your app to get what they do need.

Tip An app can update its tile only when it is running. In Chapter 5, I detail the Metro app life cycle, and you will learn that Metro apps are put into a suspended state when the user switches to another app. This means that you can't provide updates in the background. Windows 8 supports a push model where you can send XML updates from the cloud, but this service isn't available for the Consumer Preview.

Improving Static Tiles

The simplest way to improve the appearance of your application in the Start menu is to change the images used for your app's tile. You should customize the images for your app, even if you don't use any other tile features.

To do this, you will need a set of three images of specific sizes: 30x30 pixels, 150x150 pixels, and 310x150 pixels. These images should contain the logo or text you want to display but be other-wise transparent. I used a barcode motif for my example app, creating images called `tile30.png`, `tile150.png`, and `tile310.png` and placing them in the `images` folder of my Visual Studio project.

To apply the new images, open the `package.appxmanifest` file from the Solution Explorer. There is a Tile section on Application UI tab that has options to set the logo, wide logo, and small logo. There are hints to explain which size is required for each option. You will also have to set the background color that will be used for the tile; I set mine to the same color I use for the body element of my app.

Tip It is important to set the background color in the manifest, rather than include a back-ground in the images. When you update a tile, which I demonstrate in the next section, the image is replaced with dynamic information, on a backdrop of the color specified in the manifest.

You may have to uninstall your Metro app from the start screen for the tile images to take effect. The next time you start your app from Visual Studio, you should see the new static tile. You can toggle between the standard and wide views by selecting the tile and picking the Larger or Smaller buttons from the AppBar. You can see the square and wide tile formats for the exam-ple application in Figure 4-2.

Figure 4-2. *The updated static wide tile*

Notice that the word *Grocer* is displayed at the bottom of the tile. I specified this text as the value for the Short Name option in the Application UI tab and selected the All Logos option for Show Name so that it is applied to both the regular and wide tiles.

Tip   You can also replace the splash screen that is shown to the user when the application is loading. There is a Splash Screen section at the bottom of the Application UI tab in which you can specify the image and the background color it should be displayed with. The image used for the splash screen must be 630x300 pixels.

Updating Tiles

For my example app, I am going to display the first few items on the grocery list. This isn't the most useful overview, but it will help demonstrate how the tile system works.

Tile updates are based on preconfigured templates, which contain a mix of graphics and text and are designed for either standard or wide tiles. The first thing you must do is pick the template you want. The easiest way to do this is to look at the API documentation for the `Windows.UI.Notifications.TileTemplateType` enumeration, which is available at `http://goo.gl/hbC7R` (I have used short URLs in this chapter because the Microsoft URLs are long and difficult to read). The template system is based on XML fragments, and you can see the XML structure for the template you have chosen at `http://goo.gl/w8cN8`. I have chosen the `tileSquareText03` template. This is for a square tile and has four lines of nonwrapping text, without any images. You can see the XML fragment that represents the tile in Listing 4-3.

Listing 4-3. *The XML Fragment for the tileSquareText03 Tile Template*

```xml
<tile>
 <visual lang="en-US">
  <binding template="TileSquareText03">
   <text id="1">Text Field 1</text>
   <text id="2">Text Field 2</text>
   <text id="3">Text Field 3</text>
   <text id="4">Text Field 4</text>
  </binding>
 </visual>
</tile>
```

The idea is to populate the text elements with information from the application and pass the result to the Metro notifications system. To demonstrate this feature, I had added a new JavaScript file to the project called tiles.js, the content of which is shown in Listing 4-4. The length of the Windows.UI.Notifications is long enough to cause layout problems for code on the printed page, so I have created a variable called tn as shorthand and assigned the namespace to it.

Listing 4-4. *The tiles.js File*

```
/// <reference path="//Microsoft.WinJS.0.6/js/base.js" />
/// <reference path="//Microsoft.WinJS.0.6/js/ui.js" />
(function () {
  "use strict";

  WinJS.Namespace.define("Tiles", {
    sendTileUpdate: function () {
      var tn = Windows.UI.Notifications;
      var xmlFragment = tn.TileUpdateManager
        .getTemplateContent(tn.TileTemplateType.tileSquareText03);

      var textNodes = xmlFragment.getElementsByTagName("text");
      var items = ViewModel.UserData.getItems();

      for (var i = 0; i < textNodes.length; i++) {
        var listItem = items.getAt(i);
        if (listItem) {
          textNodes[i].innerText = listItem.item;
        }
      }

      for (var i = 0; i < 5; i++) {
        tn.TileUpdateManager.createTileUpdaterForApplication()
          .update(new tn.TileNotification(xmlFragment));
      }
    }
  });

  var eventTypes = ["itemchanged", "iteminserted", "itemmoved", "itemremoved"];
  var itemsList = ViewModel.UserData.getItems();
  eventTypes.forEach(function (type) {
    itemsList.addEventListener(type, Tiles.sendTileUpdate);
  });
})();
```

Tip Notice that the first letter of the template name is lowercase. If you use an uppercase letter, then you will get the default template rather than the one you wanted.

Populating the XML Template

To get the template XML fragment, I call the `TileUpdateManager.getTemplateContent` method, specifying the template I want with a value from the `TileTemplateType`. This gives me a `Windows.Data.Xml.Dom.XmlDocument` object to which I can apply standard DOM methods to set the value of the `text` elements in the template. Well, sort of—because the `XmlDocument` object's implementation of `getElementById` doesn't work, I have to use the `getElementsByTagName` method to get an array containing all of the `text` elements in the XML. These elements are returned in the order they are defined in the XML fragment, so I can iterate through and set the `innerText` property of each element to one of my grocery list items.

Tip   Only three of the four text elements defined by the XML template will be visible by the user on the Start menu. The last element is obscured by the application name or icon. This is true for many of the tile templates.

Applying the Tile Update

Once I have set the content of the XML document, I use it to create the update for the application tile. I need to create a `TileNotification` object from the XML and then pass this to the update method of the `TileUpdater` object that is returned from the `TileUpdateManager.createTileUpdaterForApplication` method:

```
...
for (var i = 0; i < 5; i++) {
  tn.TileUpdateManager.createTileUpdaterForApplication()
    .update(new tn.TileNotification(xmlFragment));
}
...
```

Not all tile updates are processed properly in the Consumer Preview, which is why I repeat the notification using a `for` loop. Five seems to be the smallest number of repetitions that guarantees that an update will be displayed on the Start menu.

Applying the Tile Update

My tile update is applied in two places. As you saw in Listing 4-4, the `tiles.js` file sets up event handlers that call the `sendTileUpdate` function whenever the contents of the grocery list change. This ensures that the tile always reflects changes the user makes to the list. I also call the `sendTileUpdate` method from the `performInitialSetup` function in `default.js`, as shown in Listing 4-5.

Listing 4-5. *Updating the Tile As Part of the Application Setup*

```
...
function performInitialSetup(e) {
  WinJS.UI.processAll().then(function () {
    UI.List.displayListItems();
```

```
    UI.List.setupListEvents();
    UI.AppBar.setupButtons();
    UI.Flyouts.setupAddItemFlyout();

    ViewModel.State.bind("selectedItemIndex", function (newValue) {
      var targetElement = document.getElementById("itemDetailTarget");
      WinJS.Utilities.empty(targetElement)
      var url = newValue == -1 ? "/html/noSelection.html"
        : "/pages/itemDetail/itemDetail.html"
      WinJS.UI.Pages.render(url, targetElement);
    });

    WinJS.UI.Pages.render("/html/storeDetail.html",
      document.getElementById("storeDetailTarget"));
    Tiles.sendTileUpdate();
  });
}
...
```

Of course, since I have created a new JavaScript file, I need to link it to default.html, as shown in Listing 4-6.

Listing 4-6. *Adding the tiles.js File to default.html*

```
...
<!-- MetroGrocer references -->
<link href="/css/list.css" rel="stylesheet">
<link href="/css/flyouts.css" rel="stylesheet">
<link href="/css/default.css" rel="stylesheet">
<script src="/js/viewmodel.js"></script>
<script src="/js/ui.js"></script>
<script src="/js/pages.js"></script>
<script src="/js/tiles.js"></script>
<script src="/js/default.js"></script>
...
```

Testing the Tile Update

A couple of preparatory steps are required before I can test my updating tile. First, the Visual Studio simulator doesn't support updating tiles, which means I am going to have to test directly on my development machine. To do this, I need to change the Visual Studio deployment target to Local Machine, as shown in Figure 4-3.

The second step is to uninstall my example app from the Start menu (which you do by selecting Uninstall from the AppBar). In the Consumer Preview, there seems to be some "stickiness" where apps that have previously relied on static tiles don't process updates correctly.

With both of these steps completed, I can now start my application from Visual Studio by selecting Start Debugging from the Debug menu. When the application has started, I can make changes to the grocery list, and a pithy summary of the first three items will be shown on the start tile, as shown in Figure 4-4.

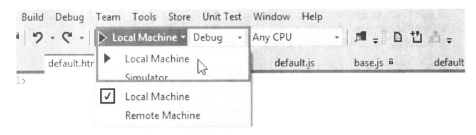

Figure 4-3. *Selecting the local machine for debugging*

Figure 4-4. *Updating an application tile*

Tip   You may not be able to find the tile on the Start menu if you have been using the simulator. If this is the case, search for the app by typing the first few letters of its name. Clicking the small search result icon will cause the tile to appear. If that doesn't work, then reboot and start the application locally, making sure not to start the simulator.

Updating Wide Tiles

The technique I showed you in the previous section is useful if you want to be able to update the square *or* the wide tile for your application. But, unless you have very specific presentation needs for your data, you should provide updates for both square and wide tiles since you have no idea which your users will select.

To update both tile sizes, you need to combine two XML templates to create a single fragment that contains both updates. In this section, I am going to combine the `tileSquareText03` and `tileWideBlockAndText01` templates. The wide template has a couple of additional fields, which I will use to display the number of stores that the user has to visit to get all of the items on the grocery list. You can see what I am aiming to produce in Listing 4-7—a fragment that follows the same format as a single template but that combines two `binding` elements.

Listing 4-7. *Composing a Single XML Fragment*

```
<tile>
  <visual lang="en-US">
    <binding template="TileSquareText03">
      <text id="1">Apples</text>
      <text id="2">Hotdogs</text>
      <text id="3">Soda</text>
```

```
      <text id="4"></text>
    </binding>
    <binding template="TileWideBlockAndText01">
      <text id="1">Apples (Whole Foods)</text>
      <text id="2">Hotdogs (Costco)</text>
      <text id="3">Soda (Costco)</text>
      <text id="4"></text>
      <text id="5">2</text>
      <text id="6">Stores</text>
    </binding>
  </visual>
</tile>
```

There is no convenient API for combining templates. The approach I have taken is to use the XML handling support to populate the templates separately and then combine them at the end of the process, which you can see in Listing 4-8.

Listing 4-8. *Producing a Single Update for Square and Wide Tiles*

```
...
WinJS.Namespace.define("Tiles", {
  sendTileUpdate: function () {

    var storeCounter = { count: 0 };
    ViewModel.UserData.getItems().forEach(function (listItem) {
      if (!storeCounter[listItem.store]) {
          storeCounter[listItem.store] = true;
          storeCounter.count++;
      }
    });

    var tn = Windows.UI.Notifications;
    var squareXmlFragment = tn.TileUpdateManager
      .getTemplateContent(tn.TileTemplateType.tileSquareText03);
    var wideXmlFragment = tn.TileUpdateManager
      .getTemplateContent(tn.TileTemplateType.tileWideBlockAndText01);

    var squareTextNodes = squareXmlFragment.getElementsByTagName("text");
    var wideTextNodes = wideXmlFragment.getElementsByTagName("text");
    var items = ViewModel.UserData.getItems();

    for (var i = 0; i < squareTextNodes.length; i++) {
      var listItem = items.getAt(i);
      if (listItem) {
        squareTextNodes[i].innerText = listItem.item;
        wideTextNodes[i].innerText = listItem.item + " (" + listItem.store + ")";
      }
    }

    wideTextNodes[4].innerText = storeCounter.count;
    wideTextNodes[5].innerText = "Stores";

    var wideBindingElement = wideXmlFragment.getElementsByTagName("binding")[0];
    var importedNode = squareXmlFragment.importNode(wideBindingElement, true);
```

```
var squareVisualElement = squareXmlFragment.getElementsByTagName("visual")[0];
squareVisualElement.appendChild(importedNode);
for (var i = 0; i < 5; i++) {
  tn.TileUpdateManager.createTileUpdaterForApplication()
    .update(new tn.TileNotification(squareXmlFragment))
}
}
});
…
```

The wider format tile gives me an opportunity to present more information to the user on each line. In this case, I include information about which store an item is to be purchased from in addition to the overall number of store visits required.

Combining templates isn't a difficult process to master, but you have to take care when trying to merge the two XML fragments. I have used the template for the square tile as the basis for my combined update. When I add the binding element from the wide template, I have to first import it into the square XML document, like this:

```
var importedNode = squareXmlFragment.importNode(wideBindingElement, true);
```

The importNode method creates a new copy of my wide binding element in the context of my square document. The arguments to the importNode method are the element I want to import and a value indicating whether I want child nodes to be imported as well (which, of course, I do). Once I have created this new element, I insert it into the square XML using the appendChild element:

```
squareVisualElement.appendChild(importedNode);
```

The result is the combined document I showed you in Listing 4-7. You can see the appearance of both tile sizes in Figure 4-5. (You can toggle between the square and wide versions by selecting the tile and using the Start menu AppBar.)

Figure 4-5. *Updating a wide tile*

Applying Badges

Metro manages to pack a lot of features into tiles, including support for *badges*, which are small icon or numeric overlays for a tile. The latter fall into the tile-as-an-advert category because there are very few situations in which a numeric representation does anything other than invite the user to start the app.

Tip Although I show tiles and badges being used together, you can apply badges directly to static tiles.

To demonstrate badges, I am going to show a simple indicator based on the number of items in the grocery list. Listing 4-9 shows the additions to the tiles.js file.

Listing 4-9. *Adding Support for Tile Badges*

```javascript
/// <reference path="//Microsoft.WinJS.0.6/js/base.js" />
/// <reference path="//Microsoft.WinJS.0.6/js/ui.js" />

(function () {
  "use strict";

  WinJS.Namespace.define("Tiles", {

    sendBadgeUpdate: function () {

      var itemCount = ViewModel.UserData.getItems().length;

      var tn = Windows.UI.Notifications;
      var templateType = itemCount ? tn.BadgeTemplateType.badgeGlyph
        : tn.BadgeTemplateType.badgeNumber;

      var badgeXml = tn.BadgeUpdateManager.getTemplateContent(templateType);
      var badgeAttribute = badgeXml.getElementsByTagName("badge")[0];
      badgeAttribute.setAttribute("value",
        itemCount > 3 ? "alert" : itemCount);

      for (var i = 0; i < 5; i++) {
        var badgeNotification = new tn.BadgeNotification(badgeXml);
        tn.BadgeUpdateManager.createBadgeUpdaterForApplication()
          .update(badgeNotification);
      }
    },

    sendTileUpdate: function () {
      // ...code removed for brevity...
    }
  });

  var eventTypes = ["itemchanged", "iteminserted", "itemmoved", "itemremoved"];
  var itemsList = ViewModel.UserData.getItems();
  eventTypes.forEach(function (type) {
    itemsList.addEventListener(type, function () {
      Tiles.sendTileUpdate();
      Tiles.sendBadgeUpdate();
    });
  });
})();
```

Badges work in a similar way to tile notifications. You obtain an XML template, populate the content, and use it to present some information to the user via the Start menu. Two types of badge template are available. The first will display a numeric value between 1 and 99, and the second will display a small image from a limited range defined by Windows.

The numeric and iconic templates are the same in the Consumer Preview and, as Listing 4-10 shows, are much simpler than the ones I used for tiles.

Listing 4-10. *The Template for Numeric and Image Badges*

```
<badge value=""/>
```

The objective is to set the `value` attribute to either a numeric value or the name of an icon. I display a numeric badge if there are three or fewer items on the grocery list. If there are more than three items, then I use an icon to indicate that the user should be concerned about the extent of their shopping obligations.

The process for creating a badge begins with selecting a template. The two template types are `Windows.UI.Notifications.BadgeTemplateType`: for numeric badges you use the `badgeNumber` template, and for icons you use the `badgeGlyph` template. You could use the same template in both situations because they return the same XML, at least in the Consumer Preview. This may change in later releases, so it is prudent to select the right template, even though the content is the same.

The next step is to locate the `value` attribute in the XML and assign it either a numeric value or the name of an icon. The numeric range for badges is very specific; it is from 1 to 99. If you set the value to less than 1, the badge won't be displayed at all. Any value greater than 99 results in a badge showing 99.

The list of icons is equally prescriptive. You cannot use your own icons and must choose from a list of ten that Windows supports. You can see a list of the icons at http://goo.gl/YoYee. For this example, I have chosen the `alert` icon, which looks like an asterisk. Once the XML is populated, you create a new `BadgeNotification` object and use it to post the update. As with tiles, I find that not all badges updates are processed, so I repeat the update five times to make sure it gets through:

```
...
for (var i = 0; i < 5; i++) {
  var badgeNotification = new tn.BadgeNotification(badgeXml);
  tn.BadgeUpdateManager.createBadgeUpdaterForApplication().update(badgeNotification);
}
...
```

All that remains is to ensure that my badge updates are created. To do this, I have changed the event handler for the grocery list events so that the tile and badge are updated together. You can see the four different badge/tile configurations in Figure 4-6, wide and square tiles, with number and icon badges.

Figure 4-6. *Displaying a badge on a tile*

Summary

In this chapter, I showed you how to adapt to Metro snapped and filled layouts and how to use tiles to provide your users with enticements to run your app or the data they require to avoid doing so. These features are essential in delivering an app that is integrated into the broader Metro experience.

You may feel that the amount of space available in a snapped layout is too limited to offer any serious functionality, but with some careful consideration, it is possible to focus on the essence of the service that you offer and omit everything else. If all else fails, you can present an information-only summary of your app and rely on JavaScript to break out of the layout.

Careful consideration is also required to get the most from tiles and badges. Well-thought-out badges can significantly improve the attractiveness or utility of your app, but ill-considered tiles are annoying or just plain useless.

Life-Cycle Events

In this, the final chapter in this book, I show you how to take control of the Metro app life cycle by responding to key Windows events. I show you how to fix the code that Visual Studio adds to projects, how to properly deal with your app being suspended and resumed, and how to implement contracts that tie your app into the wider user experience that Windows 8 offers. Along the way, I'll demonstrate the use of the geolocation feature and show you how to set up and manage a recurring asynchronous task. Table 5-1 provides the summary for this chapter.

Table 5-1. *Chapter Summary*

Problem	Solution	Listing
Ensure that your app receives the suspending and resuming events.	Subscribe to events from the `Windows.UI.WebUI.WebUIApplication` object.	1
Create a recurring background task.	Use the WinJS Promise object as a wrapper around other asynchronous activities.	2, 3
Request more time before your app is suspended.	Call the `suspendingOperation.getDeferral` method on the event passed to your `suspending` handler function.	4
Implement a contract.	Declare the contract in the manifest and respond to the type information in the `activation` event.	5, 6

Dealing with the Metro Application Life Cycle

In Chapter 1, I showed you the skeletal code that Visual Studio placed into the `default.js` file to give me a jump-start with my example project. This code handles the Metro application *life-cycle events*, ensuring that I can respond appropriately to the signals that the operating system is sending me. There are three key stages in the life of a Metro app.

The first stage, *activation*, occurs when your application is started. The Metro runtime will load and process your content and JavaScript and signal when everything is ready. It is during activation that I generate the dynamic content for my example app, for example.

Users don't typically close Metro apps; they just move to another application and leave Windows to sort things out. This is why there are no close buttons or menu bars on a Metro UI. A Metro app that is no longer required is moved into the second stage and is *suspended*. While suspended, no execution of the app code takes place, and there is no interaction with the user.

If the user switches back to a suspended app, then the third stage occurs: the application is *restored*. The app is displayed to the user, and execution of the app resumes. Suspended applications are not always restored. If the device is low on memory, for example, Windows may simply terminate a suspended app.

Correcting the Visual Studio Event Code

Unfortunately, the code for handling the life-cycle events that Visual Studio adds to a project doesn't work. It deals with activation and suspension quite happily, but it prevents the application from being notified when it is being restored. Fortunately, there are several points in the WinJS and Windows API where I can register to receive the life-cycle events, so my first task in this chapter is to update default.js so that I am properly notified when my app enters all three life-cycle stages. You can see the changes in Listing 5-1.

Listing 5-1. Registering for Life-Cycle Event Notifications

```
(function () {
  "use strict";

  Windows.UI.WebUI.WebUIApplication.addEventListener("activated",
performInitialSetup);
  Windows.UI.WebUI.WebUIApplication.addEventListener("resuming", performResume);
  Windows.UI.WebUI.WebUIApplication.addEventListener("suspending",
performSuspend);

  function performInitialSetup(e) {
    WinJS.UI.processAll().then(function () {

      UI.List.displayListItems();
      UI.List.setupListEvents();
      UI.AppBar.setupButtons();
      UI.Flyouts.setupAddItemFlyout();

      ViewModel.State.bind("selectedItemIndex", function (newValue) {
        var targetElement = document.getElementById("itemDetailTarget");
        WinJS.Utilities.empty(targetElement)
        var url = newValue == -1 ? "/html/noSelection.html"
          : "/pages/itemDetail/itemDetail.html"
        WinJS.UI.Pages.render(url, targetElement);
      });

      WinJS.UI.Pages.render("/html/storeDetail.html",
        document.getElementById("storeDetailTarget"));

      Tiles.sendTileUpdate();
      Tiles.sendBadgeUpdate();
    });
  }

  function performResume(e) {
    WinJS.Utilities.query("#topRightContainer h1")[0].innerText="Resumed";
  }
```

```
  function performSuspend(e) {
    WinJS.Utilities.query("#leftContainer h1")[0].innerText ="Suspended";
  }
})();
```

I have used the events provided through the Windows.UI.WebUI.WebUIApplication class, and they neatly map to the life-cycle events. My example Metro app doesn't currently perform any tasks that are affected by the application being suspended and resumed, but I want to show you how to test for the events. To that end, I have added statements to the performResume and performSuspend functions that change the value of h1 elements in the HTML document to indicate when the suspending and resuming events are received.

Testing the Life-Cycle Events

The most important thing to remember when testing for the resuming and suspending events is that you can't do it using the Visual Studio debugger, which disables these events so that Windows doesn't suspend your application when the debugger breaks on an exception.

This is why I have used the h1 elements to indicate when the suspending and resuming events are received. I can't use the JavaScript console or the debugger output because neither is available.

Tip   I show you how to use trigger the life-cycle events manually in the sections that follow, which means working without the debugger. There are some buttons that appear on the Visual Studio toolbar to simulate the life-cycle events *with* the debugger, but I recommend you use these with caution, because they generate simulated events that don't give you a complete picture of how your app is treated by the operating system during its life cycle.

Activate the Application

To trigger the activated event, start the application by selecting Start Without Debugging from the Visual Studio Debug menu. You can also start the app from the Start menu, either in the simulator or on your local machine. The important thing is not to start the app with the debugger.

Suspend the Application

The easiest way to suspend the application is to switch to the desktop by pressing Win + D. Open the Task Manager, right-click the item for your Metro app, and select Go to Details from the pop-up menu. The Task Manager will switch to the Details tab and select the WWAHost.exe process that is responsible for running the app. After a few seconds, the value shown in the Status column will change from Running to Suspended, which tells you that Windows has suspended the app. The app will have been sent the suspending event, but we have no way to see that until we resume it.

Resuming the Application

Switching back to the application will resume it. You will see that the h1 elements displayed at the top of the layout show that both the resuming and suspending events were sent by Windows, as shown in Figure 5-1.

Figure 5-1. *Using the DOM to report when the suspending and resuming events are received*

The state of a resumed application is exactly as it was at the moment it was suspended. Your layout, data, event handlers, and everything else will be just as it was. You don't have to call processAll when handling the resuming event, for example.

Your application could have been suspended for a long time, especially if the device was put into a low-power state (such as sleeping). Network connections will have been closed by any servers you were talking to (which is why you should close them explicitly when you get the suspending event) and will have to be reopened when your application is resumed. You will also have to refresh data that may have become stale. This includes location data, since the device may have been moved during the period your app was suspended.

Tip Windows allows users to terminate Metro apps by pressing Alt + F4. I am not certain that this feature will survive to the final version of Windows 8, but it is something you may need to consider for your app. There is no helpful warning event that gives you the opportunity to tidy up your data and operations. Instead, Windows just terminates your application's process.

Adding a Background Activity

Now that I have confirmed that my app can get and respond to the resuming and suspending events, I can add some functionality that requires a recurring background task. For this example, I am going to use the geolocation service to report on the current device location. To do this, I have created a new JavaScript file called location.js, the contents of which are shown in Listing 5-2.

Listing 5-2. *Tracking the Device Location*

```
/// <reference path="//Microsoft.WinJS.0.6/js/base.js" />
/// <reference path="//Microsoft.WinJS.0.6/js/ui.js" />

(function () {
  "use strict";

  var currentPromise;
  var tracking = false;

  function trackLocation() {
    currentPromise = new WinJS.Promise(function (complete) {
      var geo = new Windows.Devices.Geolocation.Geolocator();
```

```
    if (geo) {
        geo.getGeopositionAsync().then(function (position) {
            WinJS.xhr({
                url: "http://nominatim.openstreetmap.org"
                    + "/reverse?format = json&lat="
                    + position.coordinate.latitude
                    + "&lon=" + position.coordinate.longitude
            }).then(function (data) {
                var dataObject = JSON.parse(data.response);
                if (dataObject.address.road) {
                    var date = new Date();
                    var time = date.getHours() + ":" + date.getMinutes()
                        + ":" + date.getSeconds();
                    document.getElementById("geo").innerText =
                        dataObject.address.road + " (" + time + ")";
                }
            });
        });
    }
    complete();
    });

    currentPromise.then(function () {
        if (tracking) {
            setTimeout(trackLocation, 5000);
        }
    });
}

WinJS.Namespace.define("Location", {
    startTracking: function () {
        tracking = true;
        trackLocation();
    },

    stopTracking: function () {
        tracking = false;
        return currentPromise;
    }
});
})();
```

Using Location Tracking

The Windows 8 geolocation service is available through the `Windows.Devices.Geolocation.`
`Geolocator` object. You can subscribe to receive events when the location information changes,
but I want to demonstrate a repeating background task, so I have used the `getGeopositio-`
`nAsync` method, which produces a snapshot of the current location. This is an asynchronous
operation, and so the `getGeopositionAsync` method returns a `Promise` object that completes
when the location information is available.

When I get the location data, I make an Ajax call using the WinJS.xhr object, which is a Promise wrapper around the standard browser XmlHttpRequest object. My Ajax request is to a reverse geocoding service, which allows me to translate the latitude and longitude information from the geolocation service into a street address. The geocoding service returns a JSON string, which I parse into a JavaScript object from which I read the street so that I can display it to the user, along with a timestamp indicating the last location update.

Tip　I have used the OpenStreetMap geocoding service because it doesn't require a unique account token. This means you can run the example without having to create a Google Maps or Bing Maps account.

I have added some simple elements to the default.html file so that I can display the location to the user. You can see the additions in Listing 5-3.

Listing 5-3.　Adding Elements to default.html to Display Location Information

...

```
<script src="/js/tiles.js"></script>
<script src="/js/location.js"></script>
<script src="/js/default.js"></script>
</head>
<body>
  <div class="midtitle"><h2>Your location is: <span id="geo"></span></h2></div>
  <div id="contentGrid">
    <div id="leftContainer" class="gridLeft">
      <h1 class="win-type-xx-large">Grocery List</h1>
```

...

Tip　One of the pleasures of working with Metro using HTML5 and JavaScript is that you can choose between the HTML5 and Windows APIs for some key areas of functionality, including geolocation. I have used the Windows API in this example, but the HTML5 equivalent would have worked just as well.

Controlling the Task

I am describing the geolocation and Ajax requests only in passing because the point of this example is the creation of a periodically repeating background task. It doesn't really matter what the task does. The most important part of the location.js file is the startTracking and stopTracking functions. When I call the startTracking function, I create a new Promise object that represents the overall background task.

Tip   I have used the `Promise` object as a wrapper around the two `Promise` objects representing the request for location data and the subsequent Ajax request. When both my inner
`Promise` objects have finished, I call the `complete` function, which is passed to the callback
function I used when I created the `Promise` object. See the API reference for more information
about the `WinJS.Promise` object.

Each time the request completes, I create another `Promise` encapsulating a new request,
repeating as long as the `tracking` variable is `true`. I start a new request cycle every five seconds.

When I call the `stopTracking` function, I set the `tracking` variable to `false` and return the
`Promise` representing the current request cycle. The `Promise` I return represents a request cycle
in one of two states. The first state is when the request is active, meaning that I am waiting for
the geolocation data or the Ajax request to complete, or I am applying an update to the DOM.
If you call the `then` method on an active `Promise`, the callback function won't be executed until
the cycle is complete. The second state is when the request is complete and I am in the lull
before the next cycle starts. Calling the `then` method on a completed `Promise` will cause the
callback function to be executed without delay.

With this in mind, I am able to integrate my background task into `default.js` using the
handlers for the different life-cycle events, as shown in Listing 5-4.

Listing 5-4. *Using the Life-Cycle Events to Control a Background Task*

```
(function () {
  "use strict";

  Windows.UI.WebUI.WebUIApplication.addEventListener("activated",
performInitialSetup);
    Windows.UI.WebUI.WebUIApplication.addEventListener("resuming", performResume);
    Windows.UI.WebUI.WebUIApplication.addEventListener("suspending",
performSuspend);

  function performInitialSetup(e) {
    WinJS.UI.processAll().then(function () {

      UI.List.displayListItems();
      UI.List.setupListEvents();
      UI.AppBar.setupButtons();
      UI.Flyouts.setupAddItemFlyout();

      ViewModel.State.bind("selectedItemIndex", function (newValue) {
        var targetElement = document.getElementById("itemDetailTarget");
        WinJS.Utilities.empty(targetElement)
        var url = newValue == -1 ? "/html/noSelection.html"
          : "/pages/itemDetail/itemDetail.html"
        WinJS.UI.Pages.render(url, targetElement);
      });

      WinJS.UI.Pages.render("/html/storeDetail.html",
        document.getElementById("storeDetailTarget"));
```

```
        //Tiles.sendTileUpdate();
        //Tiles.sendBadgeUpdate();

        Location.startTracking();
      });
    }
    function performResume(e) {
      Location.startTracking();
    }
    function performSuspend(e) {
      var promise = Location.stopTracking();
      if (promise) {
        var deferral = e.suspendingOperation.getDeferral();
        promise.then(function () {
          deferral.complete();
        });
      }
    }
})();
```

The changes for the activated and resuming events are simple: in both cases I want to start my background task, so I just have to call the Location.startTracking method. The interesting part of this listing, and the reason that I included the example in this chapter, is how I handle the suspending event.

■ **Tip** Notice I have commented out the lines that apply the tile and badge updates. This is so that the example app will run in the simulator. I have also disabled the event handlers in the tiles.js file.

My problem is that any background task that is active when Windows suspends my app automatically carries on when the app is resumed. Depending on where in the request cycle the task was suspended, I can expect to see an error (for example, trying to read data from a network request that timed out during suspension) or stale data (because my task was just about to update the DOM when the app was suspended).

To help work around these problems, the suspending event defines a property called suspendingOperation that returns a Windows.ApplicationModel.SuspendingOperation object. Calling this object's getDeferral method asks Windows to give your app a little more time to prepare for suspension. When you have finished winding up your background tasks, you call the complete method on the object that the getDeferral method returned, signaling to Windows that your app is now ready to be suspended.

Asking for a deferral grants an extra five seconds to prepare for suspension. This may not sound like a lot, but it is pretty generous given that Window may be under a lot of pressure to get your app out of the way to make system resources available.

■ **Caution** In the Consumer Preview, Windows will terminate a Metro app that doesn't call the complete method on the deferral object within the five-second allowance. I imagine that this will change before the final release, but it is worth paying close attention to.

Declaring the Location Capability

Apps must declare their need to access the location service in their manifest. Before running the updated app, open `package.appxmanifest`, switch to the Capabilities tab, ensure that the Location capability is checked and save the file.

Testing the Background Task

All that remains is to test that the background task is meshing properly with the life-cycle events. The easiest way to do this is with the simulator, which supports simulated location data.

Start by defining a location in the simulator (one of the buttons on the right side of the simulator window opens the Set Location dialog box into which you can enter a location).

Once you have specified a location, start the app, remembering to do so without using the debugger. After a few seconds, you will see the location information displayed at the top of the app window, as shown in Figure 5-2.

Figure 5-2. *Location information displayed as part of the MetroGrocer layout*

Switch to the desktop and use the Task Manager to monitor the app until it is suspended. While the app is suspended, use the simulator's Set Location dialog to change the location.

Tip   I have used the coordinates of the Empire State building for this example. If you want to do the same, then use the Set Location dialog to specify a latitude value of 40.748 and a longitude of -73.98.

Resume the example app. The `resuming` event will restart the background task, ensuring that fresh data is displayed.

Tip   You may have to grant permission for the simulator and the app to access your location data. There is an automated process that checks the required settings and prompts you to make the required changes to your system configuration.

Implementing the Search Contract

The `suspending` and `resuming` events are important, but I want to return to the `activated` event and show you how it can be used to get tighter integration between your app and the rest of the Metro system. To do this, I am going to implement a *contract*, which is how Windows 8 expresses some key aspects of the Metro user experience. I am going to implement the search contract, which tells Windows that my example application is capable of supporting the operating-system wide search mechanism. In the sections that follow, I'll show you how to declare support for the contract and implement the contract terms.

Declaring Support for the Contract

The first step toward implementing a contract is to update the manifest. Open the package. appxmanifest file, and switch to the Declarations tab. If you open the Available Declarations menu, you will see the lists of contracts that you can declare support for. Select Search and click the Add button. The Search contract will appear on the Supported Declarations list. Ignore the properties for the contract; they don't do anything for JavaScript Metro apps.

Handling the Search

The purpose of the search contract is to connect the operating system search system with some kind of search capability within your application. For my example app, I am going to handle search requests by iterating through the items on the grocery list and finding the first one that contains the string the user is looking for. This won't be the most sophisticated search implementation, but it will let me focus on the contract without getting bogged down in creating lots of new code to handle searches. I have added a new JavaScript file to the project called search. js, the contents of which you can see in Listing 5-5.

Listing 5-5. *Implementing a Basic Search Feature*

```
/// <reference path="//Microsoft.WinJS.0.6/js/base.js" />
/// <reference path="//Microsoft.WinJS.0.6/js/ui.js" />

(function () {
  "use strict";

  WinJS.Namespace.define("Search", {

    searchAndSelect: function (searchTerm) {
      var searchTerm = searchTerm.toLowerCase();
      var items = ViewModel.UserData.getItems();
      var matchedIndex = -1;

      for (var i = 0 ; i < items.length; i++) {
        if (items.getAt(i).item.toLowerCase().indexOf(searchTerm) > -1) {
          matchedIndex = i;
          break;
        }
      }
      ViewModel.State.selectedItemIndex = matchedIndex;
    }
  });
})();
```

In this file, I have defined a namespace called Search that contains the searchAndSelect function. This function accepts the term that the user is searching for and performs a basic case-insensitive search through the items in the view model. If there is a match, then I set the `selectedItemIndex` property in the view model, which, through the magic of binding, will cause the matched item to be highlighted and for its details to be displayed.

■ **Tip**   As with all of the other JavaScript files in my project, I have added a `script` element to `default.html`.

Implementing the Activated Event Handler

The `activated` event is used by the system to invoke the search contract, which means I have to update the way I handle this event. Previously, an `activated` event just signaled "start the app," but now I have to pay attention to the event details to figure out what I am being asked to do. Listing 5-6 shows the changes to the `default.js` file.

Listing 5-6. Determining the Activation Detail in an Event

```
(function () {
  "use strict";

  Windows.UI.WebUI.WebUIApplication.addEventListener("activated", function (e) {
    var actNS = Windows.ApplicationModel.Activation;

    if (e.previousExecutionState == actNS.ApplicationExecutionState.notRunning) {
      performInitialSetup(e);
    }

    if (e.kind == actNS.ActivationKind.search) {
      Search.searchAndSelect(e.queryText);
    }
  });

  Windows.UI.WebUI.WebUIApplication.addEventListener("resuming", performResume);
  Windows.UI.WebUI.WebUIApplication.addEventListener("suspending", performSuspend);

  function performInitialSetup(e) {
    WinJS.UI.processAll().then(function () {

      UI.List.displayListItems();
      UI.List.setupListEvents();
      UI.AppBar.setupButtons();
      UI.Flyouts.setupAddItemFlyout();

      ViewModel.State.bind("selectedItemIndex", function (newValue) {
        var targetElement = document.getElementById("itemDetailTarget");
        WinJS.Utilities.empty(targetElement)
        var url = newValue == -1 ? "/html/noSelection.html"
          : "/pages/itemDetail/itemDetail.html"
        WinJS.UI.Pages.render(url, targetElement);
      });

      WinJS.UI.Pages.render("/html/storeDetail.html",
        document.getElementById("storeDetailTarget"));
```

```
        //Tiles.sendTileUpdate();
        //Tiles.sendBadgeUpdate();

        Location.startTracking();
    });
}

function performResume(e) {
    Location.startTracking();
}

function performSuspend(e) {
    var promise = Location.stopTracking();
    if (promise) {
        var deferral = e.suspendingOperation.getDeferral();
        promise.then(function () {
            deferral.complete();
        });
    }
}
})();
```

Windows provides information about why your application has been sent the `activated` event through the `kind` property of the `Event` object passed to your handler function. The range of possible values is enumerated by `Windows.ApplicationModel.Activation.ActivationKind`. There are different kinds of activation for different contracts for printing, for opening a file, for working with a device camera, and, of course, for handling search requests. By checking the value of the `kind` property, I can discover whether the `activated` event has been sent for a search request:

```
...
if (e.kind == actNS.ActivationKind.search) {
    Search.searchAndSelect(e.queryText);
}
...
```

The search term that the user has provided is available through the event's `queryText` property. If my `activated` event has been sent for a search request, then I call the `searchAndSelect` function, passing in the `queryText` value. This has the effect of locating and selecting the first matching item in the grocery list.

Ensuring Application Setup

My technique for servicing search requests relies on the `performInitialSetup` function having been called before I call `searchAndSelect`, because I rely on the view model and its associated bindings to translate a change in the `selectedItemIndex` property into changes in the display.

The problem is that the search-related `activated` event can have two meanings. If my app is already running, the search `activated` event means just "perform this search." But, if my app isn't running, then the event means "start the app *and* perform this search." Working out which meaning I am dealing with is important. You get only one `activated` event, even if your app isn't running when the user initiated the search.

I create duplicate bindings and event handlers if I call performInitialSetup when my app is already running. All sorts of odd behaviors emerge when this happens, but the most visible problem is that the right column in the layout contains two sets of content because I end up calling the WinJS.Pages.render method too many times. By contrast, if I fail to call perform-InitialSetup when my app wasn't running, then I don't have any bindings and event handlers and I don't display any content at all.

I need to be careful to call the performInitialSetup function when my app hasn't been running and avoid calling it the function if it has. I do this by looking at the previousExecutionState property of the event passed to the activated handler function, which reports on the execution state of my app just before the activated event was sent. The range of values for this property is enumerated by Windows.ApplicationModel.Activation.ApplicationExecutionState, but the only value I care about to solve this problem is notRunning, which tells me that the app is being told to start up as well as deal with the search:

```
...
if (e.previousExecutionState == actNS.ApplicationExecutionState.notRunning) {
    performInitialSetup(e);
}
...
```

Testing the Search Contract

To test the contract, start your app. It doesn't matter if you start it with or without the debugger, and it doesn't matter if you exit or suspend the app after you start it. The key thing is to make sure it is present on the simulator.

Next, switch to the Start menu. You app, if it was still running, will be switched to the background and, after a few seconds, will be suspended. To begin a search, just start typing. You want to search for something that will make a match, so type *hot* (so that your search will match against the hot dogs item in the grocery list).

As you type, Windows will automatically begin a standard search, looking for applications whose names contain *hot*. You will see something similar to Figure 5-3, since there are no such apps in the default Windows 8 installation.

Figure 5-3. *Initiating a search*

To switch to an application-specific search, click the app's name on the list below the search box. This will send the search activated event to the app. For my example app, I have clicked the MetroGrocer item in the list, and the activated event triggers my simple search handler, the result of which can be seen in Figure 5-4.

Figure 5-4. *Performing an application-specific search*

Tip   If you start a search from the charms bar while your app is being displayed, then Windows will automatically select it from the list, focusing the initial search on your app.

Summary

In this chapter, I showed you how to use the life-cycle events to respond to the way in which Windows manages Metro apps. I described each of the key events and showed you how to use the DOM to ensure that your app is receiving and processing them correctly.

Particular care must be taken to cleanly wrap up background tasks when an app is being suspended, and I showed you how to get control of this process by requesting a suspension deferral, allowing an extra few seconds to minimize the risk of potential errors or stale data when the app is resumed.

Finally, I showed you how the `activated` event is used to signal different requests, including obligations to fulfill the contracts that bind a Metro app to the wider Windows platform. I showed you the search contract, but there are several others, and I recommend you take the time to explore them fully. The more contracts you implement, the more integrated your app becomes.

In this book, I set out to show you the core system features that will jump-start your Metro app development. I have shown you how to use data bindings, the major structural controls, how to deal with snapped and filled layouts, how to customize your application's tile, and, in this chapter, how to take control of the application life cycle. With these skills as your foundation, you will be able to create rich and expressive Metro apps and get a head start on the final release of Windows 8.

I wish you every success in your Metro development projects.

Index

Lightning Source UK Ltd.
Milton Keynes UK
UKOW042050110612

194244UK00014B/50/P